Dear Serge,

I have been part of the world of divorced and divorcing dads for four years two months and twenty days. All the emotions and pain I have felt during that time, from my loss of financial security, loss of my children, my way of life, friends and even my dignity as a person were sensitively described in *Still A Dad*.

I have been struggling to repair my life and make it meaningful, in spite of the character assassination of me as father that is plainly and simply the fact of the divorce process for the father.

After reading about what must be the description of your own journey - no one can know this who hasn't lived it - I regained my grip on hope. Not the hope I had, but a new hope, that I had a powerful place in my children's and even my ex wife's lives that was constructive and eternal.

Thank you for describing so clearly the difference between resignation/anger and acceptance, and helping me to focus on the power in what I can do.

Sincerely yours,

Edward M. Stephens, M.D.
Member, American Psychiatric Association Council on Children, Adolescents and Their Families and the American Psychiatric Association Committee on Juvenile Justice
Founder, On Step Institute For Mental Health Research

Other advance comments on *Still A Dad*:

"*Still A Dad* places the reader inside the experience… allowing us to form the insight necessary to show compassion, to find strength during periods of despair and to focus on ways we all can help."

Travis Ballard, Esq.
Past President, National Congress for Fathers and Children

"Poignant and wise, *Still a Dad* outlines both a personal odyssey and a hopeful road for those who will experience divorce and a search for parental identity. Mr. Prengel has made constructive suggestions to give children what they need post-divorce."

Kim Boedecker-Frey, CSW

"From the wounded heart of a father who always longed to parent his children into the mystery of personal life comes a passionate essay. Serge Prengel speaks for the countless fathers unseen by the cold letter of the law and for the children deprived of the strong warmth of a dad. A must-read for all the actors on the stage called divorce."

Marcel A. Duclos, M.Th., M.Ed., CCMHC, LCPC, LADC, LCS
Professor of Psychology, Jungian Psychotherapist

"*Still a Dad* offers a fresh perspective and hope for all those loving fathers who have been shut out of their children's lives."

Paul T. Finger, M.D., F.A.C.S.
Coalition to Save Our Children

"*Still a Dad* validates the pain, rage and powerlessness often experienced by divorced fathers. However, it also provides hope for a brighter future."

Mary Giuffra, Ph.D.

Certified Couples and Family and Core Energetics Therapist

"*Still a Dad* describes the pain and agony of being a divorced dad. It then rises above that to show how to be an effective parent for your child. Excellent work, Serge!"

David Levy, Esq

President, Children's Rights Council

"*Still a Dad* provides insight and guidance as to the dynamics that fathers face as non-custodial parents. This is truly a book that speaks of issues of the heart that society ignores... that for too long fathers have shied away from. Bravo, Mr. Prengel, for the honesty!"

Milton K. Louvaris

F.A.M.I.L.Y. Advocates, Family and Divorce Mediation Services

"*Still a Dad* gives voice to the intensity of feelings fathers have when what they want in disputed child custody cases seems impossible. It offers eminently practical advice on how to handle difficult situations."

A. Jayne Major, Ph.D.

Author, *Breakthrough Parenting: Moving from Struggle to Cooperation* and *Winning the Custody Wars Without Casualties*

Hooray! At long last, a book written from the father's experience of divorce and his attempts to continue to be a vital part of his children's lives. This is a great source of wisdom, knowledge and support."

Judi Price, CSW
Family Therapist

"*Still a Dad* is a must read. It is a warm and sincere account of the trials of fatherhood, with deep insight. Its focal point is that "you will always be the father". It shows how to actualize your parenting role despite the challenges and insecurities. I recommend it for fathers, as well as mothers and grandparents."

Dr. Monty N. Weinstein
Director of the Family Therapy Center for New York and Georgia, Inc.
Director of Mental Health, National Association for Fathers

"*Still a dad* is an emotional journey on the rugged terrain of divorce. It leads the reader through the thickets and brings you out scarred but safe on the other side. Reading this book will help fathers face the expectations, the pitfalls and the emotional roller-coaster they have to go through."

Howard Yagerman, JD
NYSBA Commission on Child Welfare and Juvenile Justice
NYCLA Matrimonial Section
NYSBA Family Section

ALSO BY SERGE PRENGEL

TWELVE STEPS FOR THE DIVORCED DAD

SERGE PRENGEL

STILL A DAD

THE DIVORCED FATHER'S JOURNEY

MISSION CREATIVE ENERGY
NEW YORK

Published by Mission Creative Energy, Inc.
27 W 24th Street, New York, NY 10010.

Library of Congress Catalog Card Number 98-96241

ISBN 1-892482-00-2

Printed in Canada

For

Kate and Eric

It means a lot to me to be your dad.

many thanks

to all the fathers who shared their stories with me,
one-on-one, in groups and through the web sites
where the book-in-progress evolved

many thanks

to their children,
always so vividly present in their hearts and minds,
for inspiring all these dads to do the best they can

many thanks

to the significant women in these fathers' lives
– second wives, girlfriends, sisters, mothers -
who shared their own views of this process

many thanks

to all the professionals
who have been so generously sharing
of their experience, wisdom and kindness

I am the father of a daughter as well as a son. I have become sensitive to those grammatical conventions that tend to disempower girls.

In writing this book, I considered alternating the masculine and feminine when referring to an unspecified child.

This often works well. But, in this book, it turned out to be confusing.

So, in this book, I am using the masculine when referring to a child (except when I am specifically referring to a girl).

contents

Footnotes in the text refer to the Notes and References section at the end of the book.

foreword

Diane Yale is an attorney who has been practicing family and divorce mediation since 1984. She is a past president of the Family and Divorce Mediation Council of Greater New York, an accredited member of the New York State Council on Divorce Mediation, and a practitioner member of the Academy of Family Mediators. In the capacity of board member and chair of the State Council's Legislative Committee, she was the primary author of the model "Family and Divorce Mediation Act". Ms. Yale is a member of the Section on Dispute Resolution of the American Bar Association, and has also served on the Matrimonial Law Committee and the Committee on Arbitration and Alternative Dispute Resolution of the Association of the Bar of the City of New York.

You are about to read the touching story of a man's journey into maturity as a father and a human being. It begins with a family in crisis, and details the consequences of being processed through an adversarial divorce system that fails to provide a foundation or resources that would support former spouses and their child in establishing a peaceful and harmonious life.

The author, Serge Prengel, and I started our conversations years ago, around the time when he founded the New York City Chapter of the Children's Rights Council. Frankly, the stories of the fathers he introduced me to were in a different universe from the one I was familiar with. As an attorney with a practice in divorce mediation, my clients have been self-selected to present a very different challenge.

Typically, they walk in saying, *We want a divorce from each other. However, we have both been important to our children and intend to continue to be parents together. We want joint custody. We want to construct a system to care equally and cooperatively for our children until they are able to care for themselves.* There is a moment in the course of our discussions when their faces light up as they realize that, indeed, though they are ending their marriage to each other, they can look forward to being proud grandparents together as the years pass.

These parents are likely to be in high conflict with each other. As we work out the terms of their agreement, fears, recriminations, raised voices, and tears may be felt and expressed. Yet they keep returning to their focus, which is to jointly shape a parenting plan for the good of their children, rather than to dissipate their energy in pursuing disagree-

ment. A plan sharing the joys and responsibilities of parenthood. A plan establishing goals and principles so that as new
situations arise in the future, there are guidelines in place for
decision-making. A plan identifying a forum and procedure
for resolving any future conflict that may present itself.

Each couple has the right and the obligation to choose
and to design their own journey, whatever process works for
them so that they may heal, and so that each child may
receive all the love, attention, caring and help that is available to him or her. However, by its nature, successful mediation requires that both members of the couple say "yes" and
remain committed to the individual and collaborative effort
required in following this path. Being denied its rewards
must seem all the more poignant to those who relied on having their day in court, and learned, as did the composite
"John" of this story, what a fallacy that was.

The conversations Serge and I had eventually developed
into a workshop that we offered together, on Socially
Responsible Divorce. Here participants contemplated the
meaning of qualities such as fairness, honor, self-determina-
tion, collaboration. They practiced asserting their own
interests while being respectful of their spouse's needs and
balancing the best interests of their children. There was also
discussion of how to use the available institutional options of
court, attorneys and mediators, so that the couple's concerns
would be heard and they would remain in control of the
process and the outcome.

Unfortunately, the experience of John and his family was
not this way. While in his personal journey he waged what
he considered an ultimately effective struggle to recover him-

self, each individual man, woman and child in a society should not have to rediscover the way, make the journey alone, or do it at such immense personal expense. The questions a "system" and its professionals have to continually ask and answer are: What needs do users have that are not being sufficiently attended to? What changes can be made so that separation and divorce are not so traumatic to families? How can the system and professionals collaborate to better serve clients?

So this story is also society's journey. Indeed, we are in a historical time when the public has been demanding new structures to deal with their real-life family experience and their difficulties in being processed through the adversarial system. There have been some responsive changes in the system, but clearly much more needs to be confronted and revised.

In my own journey, I have come to regard the bonds of family in a larger, more spiritual context. Whoever or Whatever has created what we call the Universe, a man and a woman who join with each other are also in a union with that creative force. When a child results from their union, then to nurture and protect that child is to perpetuate and tend to the continuation of human life on this planet.

It is a sacred relationship, there is a taking on of the divine, a path from original creation to infinity that transcends the activities and frustrations of daily life. Whether married or not, parents are joined in spirit to each other, joined to those fragile humans who will always be their children, joined to and entrusted with the holy process of creation and nurturance and being. The family bond deserves to be honored even when it is legally in dissolution. A family can be redefined and restructured and continue on.

John's story is an allegorical tale. His personal drama gives expression to a cultural inheritance that has deep, collective resonance. John's story is also an evolutionary tale. Out of his experience of anguish and despair, he has reached the sacred. Along his journey, he offers a roadmap showing where he is and where the forks in the road lead.

It took John years to ripen into the understanding that he did not have to wait for the legislature to make new laws, for a generation of judges to retire, or for his ex-spouse to become a new person - but rather that his right to be a participatory, conscious, attentive parent was secured by the depth of his own commitment to doing it. That is where he leaves us on his journey. Let us now begin from the early steps in the journey...

Diane Yale, JD

John & Jane have a child.
They both love him very much.

John & Jane are not getting along.
They fight a lot.
When John and Jane break up,
Jane says:
You don't belong in here!
Get out of the house!

John says:
I want to divorce you, not him!
The child doesn't say much
But he's all torn inside.

Jane says:
Look what you're doing to him.
Jane goes crying to the Judge.
Look what he's doing to my child.

The Judge says:
It is the best interest of the child
That the fighting stop.
John is relieved:
The Judge will get Jane to see
A child needs both parents.

But the Judge goes on:
And for the fight to end,
There is but one way.
It is that you, John, go away.

the journey

After John and Jane break up, John wants to share the parenting of their child, and Jane doesn't. They go to court. The custody fight is long and fierce. In the end, the child stays with his mother.

As you read this story, you probably feel uneasy. Such a thing couldn't possibly happen today. Maybe, a generation or two ago – when it was more the norm for the mother to stay at home with the children. But, nowadays? When some department stores put diaper-changing stations in the men's bathrooms? These days, diapers are disposable, not dads!

doe v. doe

You may think an important part of the story has been omitted. There may be something the matter with John – after all, where there's smoke, there's fire - something in his behavior, past or present, that justifies relieving him of his parental duties. Or, maybe John is a good parent, but his lawyer is grossly incompetent?

But let's say I tell you what happened in court. Let's say I tell you more about John and Jane and their child, Joey... and you start getting a sense of who they are, what their life is like... Let's say that, having heard all that, you are reassured that John is not a bad guy. Now, you'd feel that the judge's decision was really unfair.

Well, you'd be missing the point.

Because the point is not that a particular individual is being unfairly treated. The point is that, under the current divorce system, fathers are being systematically removed from their children's lives.

This book is about John, but it is not the story of any one man. It is the story of millions of fathers in this country. It is time for all to know that a divorced dad is still a dad. Time for public discourse and public policy to go beyond gender stereotypes and the fears that perpetuate them. Time to change the laws and practice of divorce in such a way that both parents can be actively involved in their children's lives after divorce.

Even though there are so many of us, we each experience the loss, the injuries and insults of divorce in isolation – which makes it hurt all the more. One purpose of this book is to validate the feelings we experience - we wouldn't be human if we didn't feel pain, anger, resentment, self-doubt, even despair... These feelings are difficult to deal with, but they are normal. There is no gain whatsoever in denying their existence.

Through all this darkness, there is a guiding light: the conviction that, regardless of circumstances, we are still our children's dads. From this comes the hope that overcomes discouragement and sustains the efforts we make to stay involved in our children's lives. This book describes the personal journey that takes us from the shock of being treated like disposable parents to rebuilding ourselves, feeling whole as individuals and as fathers.

my journey

I experienced what, for me, was a difficult divorce. This was almost a decade ago. I have since come to meet many, many people compared to whom my own troubles were relatively minor. Yet, what happened to me was enough to affect me profoundly, to propel my life into new directions.

I began to seek out the company of others who were in similar situations; I started support groups for fathers and became an activist for shared parenting.

I became deeply interested in psychotherapy, as a client, then as a student and a practitioner.

I have been struggling with pain and anger as well as questions such as: *How can I be the more of the father I want to be? More of the person I really want to be?*

Like everybody else, I have had to deal with these issues in the midst of many pressures, wishing there was a way to escape these pressures just long enough to hear myself think. I have come to understand I couldn't do so, any more than anybody else could. We make up our philosophy of life moment to moment, as we deal with life by making choices big and small.

Life is terrifying if we see it as a series of senseless struggles, a chaotic succession of obstacles hurled our way to block us or destroy us. No sooner have we managed to escape one, that another comes out of left field.

It helps to have a roadmap – a sense of what to expect and of where the road goes. My own journey became easier the moment I started to realize that I was not alone, that I could draw on the experiences of others – people I could talk to in person, as well as people throughout history who had written about dealing with adversity and life in general.

The purpose of this book is to offer such a roadmap, based on my own experience as well as those of the many fathers I have been getting to know through the years.

**part one:
the disposable dad**

Even many, many months into the divorce proceedings, John has kept hoping: *It won't happen to me. I'll continue to be very involved in my child's life. After all, I haven't tried to shirk my responsibilities, I have a track record as a good father. It's clearly in my child's best interest to keep his father in his everyday life.*

Isn't the problem actually that fathers are not involved enough? How could society possibly rebuke a father who is actually willing and able to be as involved as the child's mother?

But this is obviously not the way the system works. And John is dismissed – from a full-fledged parent, he becomes a visitation dad.

What a difference divorce makes! One moment, John is an involved parent. The next, he is told to go away from his child. He is told to let go – his efforts to stay involved are perceived as harmful to the child.

statistics

John's situation is typical of what happens to fathers.

National Center for Health Statistics 1997 statistics[1] show that:
- Mothers have sole custody in 69% of cases
- Fathers have sole custody in 9% of cases
- Joint custody accounts for 22% of cases.

a hole in the heart[2]

The place where John now lives is a couple of blocks from a playground. Whenever he walks by, John feels a lump in his throat, a flood of emotion coming up. He fights tears –grown men don't cry in public, let alone in front of playgrounds.

He feels a terrible sense of loss. It's about missing Joey, of course. But why does it come up so strongly at the playground? It's not about actually wanting to bring Joey to a playground – the child is past that age, anyway.

All these happy children, absorbed in their games, running around, laughing, screaming… In John, it brings out a lot of sadness – the feeling that something very important has been irretrievably lost. It brings up a yearning for those innocent times when Joey's happiness reflected in his parents' eyes a sense that the world was in order.

John feels pain when he thinks of Joey's loss – and then he realizes he's also grieving for his own lost innocence. He is grieving for those days when his parenting his child was so normal that he wasn't even aware of it, when there was no question in his or anybody else's mind that it would always continue this way.

a sense of loss

Divorced fathers complain about a sense of loss. It is not that they totally lose contact with their children – a typical visitation schedule will include dinner with the father every Wednesday evening, and stay-overs with the father every other week-end. But can anybody honestly say that a few visits a week is an acceptable substitute for an involved parenting relationship?

This is how Vince G. describes his experience:

I was the main caregiver in my marriage of 12 years for our 8 year old son. I became very attached to my son and he to me... My marriage began to fall apart many years ago and so many resentments surfaced for both my ex and myself. She resented my being so close to our son and missing the time with him...

I will never regret my time with my son in his formative years. Unfortunately, the residual effect is that we became so close and attached that our separation is very painful and downright overwhelming.

Fathers are complaining about the loss of being involved

in the ordinary events of their children's life. They miss the
seemingly insignificant events of everyday life – the rhythm
of waking up, breakfast, school, after-school homework, too
much TV, time to go to bed now… Once these ordinary
interactions are removed, the nature of the relationship
changes in such a palpable way, it is as if it has now lost its
texture. Father and children now interact primarily around
entertainment, not on the whole spectrum of activities that
make up the children's lives.

Take, for instance. J. W.:

*I have 2 girls 5 and 7. We had a very close relationship. They
are going to miss me very much.*

*Not being able to help them with their homework and read
them a bedtime story while sitting right next to them is going to
pain me for a long time.*

Or Al, who came to understand later in life how much it
meant to him to be an involved father:

*I have a 3 1/2 year old daughter. Divorced a little over a
year…I have four grown children and eight grandkids. At my
age of 51 I honestly never wanted more children. Amanda has
turned out to be my whole life. And seeing her every other weekend and on Wednesday evenings if I am in town, for two hours,
is simply not enough. I am just a visiting father. Quality time is
limited.*

*These youthful years that mom and dad share and bond with
the kids go fast. I missed a lot of that with my first four children
by working all the time and feeling that they were just there.
Now I am older and being divorced with Amanda so very
young, I suffer not being with her. Words cannot express that.*

Fathers need just the same amount of time to share the work and fun of the children, just the same as the mother.

There is a big loss to mourn – the loss of being with your children here and now. A day that goes by can never be replaced. It's gone.

no longer a real parent

Back to John and Jane Doe's story. Most of what Joey - their child - hears about the situation comes from his mom rather than his dad. Joey sees his mother's pain and anger – for one thing, women tend to be more prone to communicating their feelings, for another, he spends more time with her. Joey seems to be living the divorce through his mother's eyes. He thinks – and sometimes says: *Mom's a better parent, this is why I'm with her.*

Is it that Joey doesn't love his dad? No, but Joey is a child, and he tries to cope with the overwhelming complexity of the situation as best as he can.

Joey loves both his parents. How can he deal with the fact that they're no longer together, and there's a lot of animosity between them? He's still a child, he needs parenting.

A child needs certainties, simple answers, a sense that there is fairness and logic in the world, in order to feel reasonably safe. Mom's now his primary caretaker. Joey desperately needs to believe that the person on whom he depends most is a good person – loves him and cares for him.

If Mom and Dad fight, if both of them can't be good, then it must mean Mom's the good parent and Dad the problematic one. Besides, *Mom wanted Dad out of the way. The law was on her side. It probably means there's something wrong with Dad.*

This kind of logic is not just a childish trait. We all try to simplify very complex situations – situations that involve a difficult emotional conflict. This is what psychologists call removing the "cognitive dissonance": When there are elements in the situation that we cannot reconcile with what we need to believe, we tend to blot out the parts that don't fit.

As a result, John not only has to contend with the loss of time spent with his son, he also feels the loss of his son's esteem for him.

the curse of the jackass

What happens to the self-esteem of the child who sees his father being put down?

There is a cartoon by Frank Cotham – it is a caricature and, therefore, not very subtle; as a result, it provides a very poignant illustration of the ugly effect of a parent's ugly moods on a child's mind.

The mother is talking to her son. She's sitting down, looking angry or scornful. The son's standing in front of her, awkwardly, like somebody who is being scolded or who's being told unpleasant "truths". In it, the mother is saying: *Your father was a jackass.* And we see that the little boy has jackass ears and a tail!

Your father was a jackass

she calls him daddy and calls me randy

It's horrible to know that your child might feel he's bad because he's like you... It's also heartbreaking to feel you're no longer considered to be the father, as in the following story:

My daughter is 5 1/2 years old and I have been divorced since she was 6 months old... (About a year ago), I was served with papers saying that her Mom was remarried and moving to the state of Alabama... Since February of 1997 I have been driving 13 hours to the state of Alabama on the 3rd weekend of every month to see my daughter. I pick her up on Friday at 6:00 and we stay in a motel until Sunday at 6:00 p.m. and I take her back to her mothers and I drive the 13 hours back to Oklahoma.

...My daughter is convinced that he (the wife's new husband) is her Daddy and I am called Randy. That hurts more than you can imagine. I put out so much effort to be a part of her life and I get nothing in return. When I go to see her we still have so much fun together but I want to be thought of as Daddy not Randy.

...Her new step-father and I exchanged words a few months ago and he said "you're no father, you're just a sperm donor, don't forget that". I believe my ex-wife is doing everything she can to just get me to disappear from my daughter's life.

Shut up and disappear! Elie Wiesel has said there are two cruelties in torture – one is the torture itself, the second is the silence people observe about it.

crazy-making

John wants to stay actively involved in his child's life, to remain his parent – not a visitor. He wants to be involved in the events, big and small, of his day-to-day life. He wants both Jane and him to contribute fairly to the costs of raising him. He wants decisions about money to be joint decisions. He doesn't like to give over to Jane child support money without having a say over how it's spent.

But no, says the judge, *this cannot be, you are a controlling man. Go away, pay, and let the child's mother handle the parenting* (these are obviously not the specific words – but this is what they sound like to John).

In this context, control is a dirty word. It's a code word to

imply that John, as a man, is obsessed by power and control
– as opposed to the more humane, nurturing values attrib-
uted to Jane and women in general. John is seen as acting
against the best interest of the child.

power and control

According to the traditional laws of divorce, the custody
dispute is resolved to satisfy *the best interest of the child*.
Usually, the laws do not define what this *best interest* is. It is
then usually assumed that the best interest of the child is to
be in the custody of the better parent (I don't like the word
custody, but I use it because it is the legal word).

The traditional divorce is an adversarial process in which
parents are encouraged to fight it out so that "the best parent" may win.

This looks strikingly like a form of the archetypal male
ritual of fighting for dominance of the herd. Yet there is an
irony in how the roles are played.

On the one hand, we have the man, John. He is asking
that Jane and he find a way to co-parent instead of fighting
to destroy each other. In other words, he's embodying the
"feminine" attitude of cooperation.

On the other hand, Jane is claiming that she, and only
she, can be in charge. She's embodying the "masculine" attitude of competition for dominance.

The cultural stereotypes are so strong that this goes large-
ly unnoticed. Instead, John is accused of being competitive
– because he's not accepting Jane's bid for dominance!

insidious assumptions

So insidious are some assumptions that people don't notice that they are just assumptions, prejudices. Not even the people who are their victims. It takes a lot of time for society to see these assumptions for the put-downs they really are.

Take the old declaration that "Black people are less intelligent than Whites". It has taken desegregation, affirmative action, Black pride, the emergence of viable role models, to make a significant change in the devastating, belittling effects of such assumptions.

Similarly, it has taken decades for society to disbelieve such statements as "Women are less capable of working than men". And, despite all the progress we have made in this area, we are still far from being free of gender-related prejudices.

Women are still often viewed as primarily focused on nurturing, and men as primarily focused on breadwinning. These limiting beliefs are all the more damaging because they are implicit, and at odds with society's stated goal of eliminating gender biases.

One area where the contradiction between our expressed goal of gender equality and the influence of hidden biases is most striking is in divorce.

When there's a divorce, it's most likely that the children will stay with the mother. The father's main role is to pay child support, he becomes a visitor to his own children.

how this happens

It's not that the laws say of fathers: *Kick the bum out.* In fact, it's just the opposite: divorce laws are usually written in a gender-neutral style. They solemnly emphasize that their focus is *the best interest of the children.* According to the laws, either parent can be the custodial parent.

The law views the custody proceedings as *a search for the better parent* – or, to be more accurate, the elimination of the less fit parent. Now, the concept of *search for the better parent* is not a legal construct – it is just a way of describing what happens in fact during a contested divorce. So there is no legal definition of what it is that constitutes a better parent.

Essentially, this is a case of: *I can't define it, but I know one when I see one.*

And this is how the unacknowledged bias results in selecting the mother and eliminating the father.

There are people who say this is not always the case. And they have a point: after all, fathers have been getting sole custody in 9% of cases!

the logic of the system

I find it deeply disturbing to see such a discrepancy between the gender-neutral content of the laws, and the reality that custody is usually awarded to the mother. But, sad as it is to say, there's a logic to it. To understand it, just imagine for a moment you're the judge. You have in front of you two bickering people. You don't really know what's behind all the stories they tell about each other - in fact, the more you hear, the less you may be inclined to think that either parent is a decent person. Yet, you have to make a decision, choose one or the other.

It's like an election - there has to be a winner, and only one; winning is based on convincing just a little over half of the voters that you're better than your opponent.

In other words, even if both parents are equally good parents, even if the judge trusts the father's ability to be nurturing, all it takes to tilt the scales in favor of the mother is a fuzzy warm feeling about motherhood.

Aren't we all conditioned to have a warm feeling in favor of *motherhood and apple pie*? The mother is almost automatically viewed as the more nurturing parent. In the vast majority of cases, the mother is awarded custody.

What this means, in practice, is that a father only gets custody when he can prove that the mother is actually "unfit" to be a parent. This is probably why the percentage of fathers with sole custody (9% in 1994) has not changed from 20 years ago, when most states only allowed fathers to have custody if the mother was unfit. The letter of the law has changed, but the old spirit persists.

a tough situation

The assumptions underlying these practices are so solidly entrenched in our culture that, to many people, they do not seem to be assumptions, they appear to be self-evident truths. So it is important to see what these assumptions are and to point out that there are other ways of seeing things.

Dennis Guttsman[3] points out that even the language betrays our society's cultural biases. He asks: *What is the masculine of "mothering"?* There is no masculine word that captures the love and nurturing associated with "mothering". The word "fathering" as we usually use it refers more to inseminating than to providing emotional care and on-going parenting.

While the justice system makes a great show of having no gender biases whatsoever, its noble ideal of serving *the best interest of the children* in fact amounts to giving free rein to the unspoken bias that mothers are the true nurturers.

Our divorce system effectively removes fathers from their children, and turns fathers into the means of supporting single mothers.

the money trap

John is standing in front of the judge. *Let's take things in order*, says the judge. *We've dealt with custody. Now, the amount of child support. You know what the State's guidelines are. And Jane showed you what the child needs to be decently cared for.*

John is trying his best to remain calm. Inside, he's fuming, choking. It shows in his contorted face. *Calm down*, says the judge. *See how hard it is to deal with him*, says Jane.

The judge says: *I don't have all day. Are you refusing to take care of your child?*

- *No, but...*

- *Look, don't try to finagle with me. I'm an old hand at this.*

I've seen them all. Just shoot straight, and we'll lose less time.

John would like to say: *You're so hard on me. Couldn't you please show me a little heart?* Just like Jane does so well. Jane is so good at showing how much she suffers. People can see how she's affected by what's happening - everybody is convinced that the divorce is hurting her more than it's hurting John. She is also very expressive in showing how much she's affected by the child's suffering. It plays on the cliche: women are sensitive; men aren't. John is in a quandary: when he says he too is suffering, it seems to turn back against him. People either look at him like he's not very manly - or they believe he's faking it to compete against Jane. In a way, it is easier for him to keep his suffering to himself.

They – Jane, but also the court, the laws, people – don't trust John. *If he loves his child anywhere near as much as he claims to, why is he making so much trouble coming up with the money to take care of him? And why are his "explanations" so convoluted?*

The judge insists: *State your case.* The request is cold, steely. There's no sympathy in it.

- *OK. Look, it's not easy. I simply can't come up with the money. I tried. I tried, but I really can't. I was hoping I was going to be able to find a way – it would have made all our lives easier. I was hoping for a miracle. But I just can't do it.*

The Judge has been listening with a sarcastic smile on his face – *Some men will go to all ends to avoid paying child support.*

The judge tells John: *Look, you've got to pay.*

what john can't say

Why is it John is so incapable of explaining what he wants? Why is it that everything he says sounds like a pathetic effort to shirk his duties?

For one thing, there's a difficulty inherent to any adversarial situation. It's hard to state what you want when you know that, in order for you to have it, your adversary is not going to have what they want - and that they're going to fight to get their way.

Of course, Jane has a similar problem: For her, John is the adversary; and she'll only get what she wants to the extent that it is taken away from John.

But there is a major difference between John and Jane's situation. What Jane wants is considered legitimate, and what John wants isn't.

When the judge asks him to state what he wants, John has to resist the urge to shout his pain and anger: *What I want, you don't allow me to even state. I want to share parenting, I want to share expenses on an equitable basis. And you tell me it is not even an option unless Jane agrees to it of her own will.*

John knows this kind of outburst would not get him anywhere with the judge. So he tries his best to be constructive, to work within the system, to find permissible alternatives to what he really wants. But how can he find a way to express the desire to be an equal parent within a system that only allows a one-up/one-down outcome to a custody dispute?

This system views things in terms of custody and visitation when John yearns for a benevolent authority to allocate

parenting time between equally respected parents. The system focuses on child support, when John yearns for parental
responsibilities to be equitably allocated.

John's words betray him, because the system has no room
for what he wants, no acceptable words for that. His emotions remain all choked up inside. And the more it goes, the
more he looks to Jane and the judge like somebody who is
just trying to justify the unjustifiable- somebody whose only
goal is to pay as little as he can get away with.

guidelines

Of course, the system is right to expect a father to be
financially responsible for his child. All parents should be,
whether they are married or not, whether they are fathers or
mothers. But the way money is dealt with in a traditional
divorce makes fathers feel even more "divorced" from their
children.

The system is based on guidelines defined by the states'
legislatures, specifying what percentage of the non-custodial
parent's income must be paid to the custodial parent as child
support.

The child support guidelines were created to protect
mothers and their children from the fathers who abandon
them. They address very real problems, depicted dramatically and often in the media. We are all familiar with the plight
of teenage mothers struggling to raise kids while barely out
of childhood themselves - this appeals to our compassion.
We have also heard a lot about the "welfare mothers" supported by taxpayers when the fathers could be picking up the

tab – this appeals to our desire for fiscal restraint.

This, in itself, is not the problem. In fact, it is wonderful that, as a society, we want to take care of the major social problem of fatherless families. And it's only fair that we want to find ways to get irresponsible fathers to act responsibly.

What's unfortunate is the effect that the laws and guidelines have on fathers like John. Simply because he is a divorcing father, John is automatically treated like somebody who wants to abandon his child. There is an assumption that the mother will continue to be loving and responsible, whereas the father will have to be coerced into doing the right thing. The mother remains in charge of deciding what to buy for the children, and the father has to make child support payments. That a father may have a loving interest in doing the best for his child is not even remotely in the picture – except, yes, if he really wants his child to have things the mother won't buy, why doesn't he just pay for them, in addition to the regular child support money?

The point is: the child support guidelines have nothing to do with the situation of fathers like John, who are struggling to remain actively involved in their children's lives. Applying such an approach to a father like John is only adding insult to injury – contributing to the sense of betrayal and isolation that he feels as he sees his parental role taken away from him.

harsh realities

Divorcing parents are not obligated to follow the guidelines – provided they both agree to another arrangement. When they don't is when the guidelines take effect. Now, this seems fair – in the sense that both parties have an equal opportunity to disagree. In practice, what this means is that the mother has no incentive to make an effort to work out a mutually agreeable way to deal with parenting expenses: she knows that she is likely to get child support payments that she can use as she sees fit.

Society tends to be sympathetic to the plight of the mother . The media tell us about divorced mothers who find it very difficult to maintain a lifestyle comparable to what they had when they were married.

But… if things are hard for mothers, it doesn't mean they are easy for fathers. What happens with divorce is that the family's expenses are much higher while the income usually isn't. Two households are created when there used to be one. Housing costs alone already accounted for a high percentage of the family's budget before divorce; and now there are two homes to maintain.

Stories that show us mothers living less well after divorce are misleading – because the implication is that it is the father's fault. The harsh reality is that divorce significantly affects *both* parent's lifestyles. In fact, after factoring in child support payments, many fathers end up being much worse off financially than their ex-wives, as we'll see in the following.

income shifts

Depending on the state where he lives, a father must pay 15% to 20% of his *pretax* income (20% to 25% after-tax) as child support for one child. This goes to 25% to 35% pretax

(30% to 40% after-tax) for more children.

The effect of these payments is to shift *tax-free* income to the mother – while alimony/maintenance is tax-deductible, child support is not. Conversely, the father's after-tax income is dramatically reduced, as can be seen in the following example.

This is the case of a middle-class family with two children. The father's income is $3,000 a month, and the mother's income is $1,500 a month. The father pays typical child support that is 25% of his pre-tax income. The following chart shows how much money each parent actually has to spend each month, after taking into account child support and taxes.

	father	mother
Monthly gross income	3,000	1,500
Child support	-750	+750
Income taxes - fed, state & local after deductions & exemptions	-1,050	-100
Net monthly income	1,200	2,150

In addition to child support per se, the father may be required to pay for additional expenses (all or part of health insurance, day care, etc). In some states, he may also have to contribute to mortgage payments. For instance, in Maryland, the custodial parent gets use and possession of the family's house for three years – with the non-custodial parent required to pay half or all of the mortgage during that period on top of child support.

Even without these additions, the father is left with $1,200 a month, and the mother with $2,150.

The point of this example is not to say that the mother is better off after divorce than she was before – she probably has a harder time making ends meet. The point is that neither the father nor the mother is doing well. Unfortunately, the adversarial divorce exacerbates the situation by wasting both parents' resources in legal battles. In addition, it creates a mentality of "me first" instead of "how can we conserve the limited resources we have".

Society tends to focus on the divorced mother's financial woes, and not to see the father's. If it is difficult for the mother to maintain a household for $2,150 a month, how much more difficult for the father to do so on $1,200 a month!

After paying child support, this father has no money left to get a home where his children can feel at home with him. This makes a mockery of joint legal custody – in which the mother receives the same amount of child support as if she had sole custody.

the plight of the involved father

The child support guidelines define child support amounts based on income. They usually do not take into consideration whether or not the child is actually spending time with the father – which creates additional costs for the father. For instance, it costs the same to have a room for your children in your home, whether they use it one night a week or seven nights a week.

As a result, a father who wants to stay involved with his children not only has to support the child's expenses at his mother's, he also has to find a way to pay for the child's expenses when he's with him.

Two households are more expensive to maintain than one. Unfortunately, most of the current laws and guidelines place this burden primarily on the father's shoulders.

Here's what stepmother Elizabeth P. has to say about this:

My husband has two children by an earlier marriage.

He pays child support faithfully and on time; he pays for medical and dental insurance for the children; he pays for a life insurance policy that will go to his children (it will remain in effect until the youngest is 21).

He pays for half of the uncovered medical and dental bills, eyeglasses, and contact lenses. He pays part of their tuition. And then there are the expenses related to "visitation."

From the time their parents divorced when the oldest child was two years old until they were in their late teens - and school, social life, and weekend jobs got in the way - my stepchildren lived in our house EVERY weekend, one evening a week, part of the summer, and some holidays.

Like their mother, we also had to provide a home for them. Our expenses related to the children included: food (a whopper of a bill when they were teenagers; we also fed many of their friends on weekends); phone (also a whopper), gas, electricity, water, bedroom furniture, linens, VCR and TV for their room, toiletries (toothpaste, toothbrushes, combs, brushes, deodorant, contact lens solution, shampoo, conditioner, acne medicine, cough medicine, toilet paper, etc.), clothing, books, magazines, toys, school supplies, games, sporting equipment, birthday gifts,

*Christmas gifts, summer vacations, allowances, transportation
(including 5000 miles a year to drive them between our house
and their mother's), sporting events, movies, concerts, babysit-
ters...I think you get the picture.*

gripes about money

Money issues, as many marriage counselors say, are symp-
toms of power struggles within the couple. In a divorce situation, the issue is further clouded by a tremendous amount
of guilt and blame that's placed around it.

A married man is presumed to be an equal partner to his
wife in budgeting child-related expenses. A divorced man is
required to make substantial pre-set payments to his ex-wife,
without any say whatsoever in how the money is used.

The laws of divorce claim to be geared to fairness and rea-
sonableness. Yet, from a father's point of view, the result feels
quite unfair - winner takes all, humiliates the loser, and does
it all in the name of the best interest of the child.

Fathers feel that the burden of the additional expenses
due to divorce is disproportionately placed on their shoulders. They find it unfair that the payment of child support
to the mother is justified by her being involved in raisin the
children; but, if the father wants to get more involved, he has
to pay even more money.

It is a heavy burden – and the sheer weight of it, in addition to the lack of recognition fathers get for carrying it –
contribute to a sense of despair.

from bad to worse

Not only is Jane not interested in shared parenting, she seems to be sabotaging every attempt John makes in this direction. Worse even, at times she seems bent on pushing him away from his own son's life.

The visitation schedule makes a joke out of being a father, says John. *I'm becoming some kind of an uncle to my son. It's so obvious that now, for him, his mother is the real parent. I know how to be a father - I don't know how to be a visitor to my son.*

As if this weren't enough, Jane seems to have no respect for John's parenting time. She withholds visitation whenever she wants, for the flimsiest of reasons. When John thinks about this, he feels a rising tide of outrage.

access

Even if the father is granted significant visitation rights, the custodial mother effectively controls the time, place and manner of his visits with the children. Sanford Braver's study[4] shows that visitation denial is a problem in about 25% of divorces.

In practice, there is not much effective recourse for fathers to prevent custodial mothers from interfering with the access to the children or from turning the children against them. The power struggle will then continue - or even escalate – well after the divorce is finalized. Take, for instance, Cecil's case:

My ex-wife allows me to speak with my daughter ONLY when she returns my calls collect. I have had no Holidays, vacations or Birthday celebrations for 2 years with my daughter. I have only seen my daughter ONE time in this last year, and the child's paternal grandparents and uncles and aunts NONE, although when we were married they saw her regularly.

There is, in theory, legal recourse for the father. But what many fathers actually find out is that the courts will not – or cannot - do much to really help them in this area. A court action by the father rarely succeeds unless the mother's conduct is egregious over long periods of time and can be verified by others. Says Robert H.:

After paying my child support in a timely manner and being refused visitation by my wife, I have come to the point that the family law system is not working for the good of children.

Here's William R's story:

I have been without "reasonable visitation" for over 5 years now. The courts are no help, I can't afford an attorney, and basically I am at the mercy of my ex-wife. She has new cars, new home, moved out of the state, and lives a high life. I on the other hand, am without my children for periods of time that range from six months to over a year. I work 50 to 70 hours per week, to make ends meet. If I didn't have the support (emotionally or financially— sad to say, isn't it?) of my fiancée, I'd be living on the streets.

descent into despair

You lose your child – You're told you don't have the right to be a full-fledged parent, just a visitor. You're told your role is not to nurture, it is to pay.

You feel hurt, humiliated and angry.

You try to fight, but everything you do seems not to work – or, actually, to work against you. You lose faith in the system, and even in yourself.

You feel like you're the powerless victim of your ex, the judge, the system. You feel overwhelmed, helpless, hopeless. You go into a spiral of despair.

torture

Giving the parental authority to the mother instead of keeping it shared between both parents was intended to avoid conflicts. Unfortunately, this is not the case. The frustration keeps growing. The father is constantly reminded of his one-down position – through his financial burden, his reduced role in the everyday life of his children, careless or acrimonious infringements on his visitation schedule, etc...

The father feels that the mother can do whatever she wants. She is torturing him, taunting him with her power. Some fathers become obsessed with the deprivation – a man possessed. Says D. T.:

My girlfriend has used the courts to prevent me from having any contact with my 5 month old daughter. We have a court appearance on Oct. 3. I need support, I can't sleep or eat, I want to see her but am prevented for no known reason.

rage

Many otherwise perfectly reasonable men go into incoherent rage when they start talking about what's happening in their divorce, as if there was a bottleneck in their throat, choking all the grievances and outrages that are struggling to come out at the same time.

For some fathers, it's easier to articulate their sense of outrage - at their ex, at the lawyers, the judge, the system... Like Joe O.:

May the Judges and Lawyers swim in the tears of the divorced fathers throughout this country. They're responsible for

letting this disgraceful system go on and on without any regard
for doing the right thing.

Some men have an almost irresistible impulse to strike
back, if not with blows, at least with hurtful words. Witness
Russ E.'s complaint:

Because of suck-ass judges and "highly reimbursed by the ex-
husband" attorneys, the children in approximately 90% of
divorces go to the mother, who is greatly rewarded for her failed
marriage with high child support, medical for the kids, 100%
day care expenses, and then whatever else the asshole judge wants
to throw in on top of that...

And, with the frustration mounting, there's the fantasy of
the ultimate revenge. Says M. F.:

The only way men are going to be with their children is for
the spouse to die. Period. Unfortunately, I suspect that is exactly
what some aggrieved men do accomplish.

Feeling abandoned by all, some curse at the society that
seems to have so little room for them. Says David C.:

I will be going to jail on December 7th because I am not
willing to cave in to the pressure of my ex-wife, the system and
a nazi-like judge.

the abyss

These stories are clearly not representative of the average
divorce. They reflect situations where something snapped –
there is no longer restraint. It's the descent into the heart-of-

darkness, indulging in destructiveness and self-destructiveness.

In that, these stories provide a dramatic picture of the extremities to which the frustrations of divorce can drive some men.

Most fathers, while not experiencing such depth of despair, get quite a taste of it. And so it is that we have a taste of how close we come to the abyss: diving into the spiral of despair, acting out our despair in rageful ways, further alienating others' sympathies, and as a result feeling ever more cut off from the rest of the world – which, in turn, contributes to our sense of growing despair.

the outcast

In the beginning, it was a private matter among peers. John and Jane disagreed - not an unusual occurrence. But, this time, they could neither resolve the issue nor sweep it under the rug. The argument took on a life of its own. John got scared of Jane. And Jane got scared of John. Whatever trust they had in each other was now replaced by hurt, fear and anger.

It's never been that easy for John and Jane to make difficult decisions together. Now, they're facing the most difficult decision they ever had to face – how their child is going to be parented.

John and Jane's fight creates a vacuum, so they go out of

the family unit to fill it. Society interferes in the fight. Society – the law, the judge – has the following message: *For this, the most important task an adult may have, a competition is set up. One of you will remain as a parent, and the other will be out. May the best parent win.*

The fight is long and hard – lawyers make enough money on it to send their own children to law school. But the result is predictable. The child stays with the mother.

escalation

The judge, the courts, the laws, society… are siding with Jane against John. They're telling John to give up being a father the way he knows to be a father. He no longer has the right to even want that.

He's feeling humiliated, vanquished. No matter what he does, no matter how smart his moves seem to be, things always have a way of turn back against him. It looks like Jane can do no wrong. Even her stupidest moves seem to always end up benefiting her. It seems like all she has to do is to say: *I'm the mother.*

Now, John is no longer just in conflict with Jane - a peer. He's in conflict with the world. The world is saying, loud and clear, that she's the better parent. Which, in this context, means: *the better person.*

John tries to say: *I'm a human being, too. I have a heart, I care for my child, I am nurturing, too.* And he's told: *Go back to the salt mines, go work, that's all you're good for.*

He is left stewing in his own juices. He has fantasies of going to Court and being vindicated – but, by now, he doesn't trust the legal system anymore.

One moment, he's mad as hell – and he realizes all too well, all too soon, it's powerless anger. The next moment, he feels down, really down and depressed.

It feels like everything and everybody is against him.

some parents are more equal

Jane might agree to shared parenting. *But, in most states, she doesn't have to*; and, if she doesn't, he's stuck. His needs, his feelings, his ideas about what works for children, are not nearly as important as hers. He's at her mercy.

Society gives Jane the power to refuse to share parenting. In too many states, shared parenting won't happen unless the mother agrees to it. Fathers may be able to obtain joint legal custody – which gives them a right to have a voice in some "big" decisions like the choice of religion or of schooling. But it leaves them out of the loop in terms of their child's everyday life. And they have no say in how the child support money is used.

And so it goes on along a predictable scenario. Jane says she doesn't want to share anything with John, least of all parenting. He hopes that if he can find the right words, she'll understand. But… the more he insists, the more determined she gets. He keeps hoping against all hope that she'll eventually see things his way. And even if she doesn't, how could the judge not understand? *There are principles we all believe in, aren't there? This is about the best interest of the child. How could Joey's best interest possibly be to lose me?*

Actually, the judge doesn't want to discuss principles. The

judge sees a situation he's familiar with – parents who dis-agree – and he has a ready "solution" for this situation. The judge just lays down the law, as he sees it.

It's really unfair, says John. Not fair: he has to submit to an overwhelming force he can't argue with, a logic that treats him as if he doesn't count.

it feels like rape

Rape is not just a sexual act; most of all, it's an act of vio-lence, an abuse of power. The rapist only sees the woman he rapes as a means to satisfy his needs, not a person who has any rights or feelings of her own.

In a milder way, this is what people experience when their house has been burglarized. Seeing how easily a burglar can come into our private space, open all doors and drawers, ran-sack through it… leaves us feeling shaken up. It makes a mockery of our view of home as a safe haven. Our sacred space has been invaded, violated.

Likewise, our right to fatherhood is violated and stolen by the divorce process. Fathers seem to be seen only as a means to the end of maintaining a family led by a single mother.

justice in the dark ages

There is something reminiscent of medieval justice in the way the courts deal with the conflict of divorce.

Back in the Middle Ages, judges would order a "judicia-ry duel", fought till death ensued, to determine which of two litigants was right. The logic was that God would intervene in favor of the righteous party. Our adversarial divorce system is essentially a judiciary duel, in which mother and father are encouraged to destroy each other in order to find out who the best parent is. Worse yet, the result of this fight is fairly predictable. Fathers rarely win.

In fact, divorce, from a father's point-of-view, is actually more like another form of medieval justice. Back then, to determine whether or not you were guilty of a major crime, you'd be subjected to a form of torture called *ordalia* (in English, *ordeal*). If you died from it, you were obviously guilty. If you were innocent, God would perform a miracle to save you. Needless to say, the odds were you'd be dead and guilty.

excluded from the human community

If you're one of these unfortunate fathers, you're out of the loop before you even had a chance to understand what was happening to you. You may feel a tremendous sense of pressure: cave in, or else. Your experience is that your child is taken away from you – yet they call you a troublemaker for resisting. They call you controlling when you want to retain some influence in your child's day-to-day life.

And it's hard to find a really sympathetic ear. People, at best, don't understand what's happening. People ask: Isn't it the way things are done? Be a good father… let the mother do the parenting, and do your job - pay child support. Or, they ask, could it just be that you are trying to skirt your financial obligations to your children?

You begin to wonder whether the whole world's gone

crazy, or whether you have. One way or another, you feel increasingly cut-off from others. Excommunicated.

From time immemorial, the harshest punishment that a tribe could inflict upon one of its wayward members was to throw him out of the community – *you're no longer part of us, go away from our fire, go wither and die all by yourself like a beast.*

**part two:
an eye-opener**

John used to feel pretty cool, very much in tune with the spirit of the times. He was doing his best to balance work and family. He'd made a place for himself in a world which views success as not just holding a good job, but also having good relationships with people, in particular with your children. He knew of women who complained that their husbands were not involved enough in the housework and in raising the children. He was feeling smug, so superior to these guys. Occasionally, he'd hear of divorced fathers who complained that they were not seeing their kids enough, that they had to give too much money to their ex. He couldn't help thinking that these men were deadbeats who probably deserved what happened to them.

Until it happened to him.

So it is that John
Is kicked out of his son's life,
Is now just a wallet for his wife.

no way, we won't pay

The divorce process is disheartening for John. Jane is so passionately bent on having her way, she seems invincible to him. She's pulling all the stops, going for a complete and total victory – to get his child, because she's the mother; his house, because the child deserves to live there; and his money, to pay for all that.

To John, it feels like a torrential outpouring, so powerful that it would be impossible to swim upstream. There's a message in Jane's rage, a message that is further amplified by what happens in court. It's a bullying message: *Give in to the torrent, or be carried away against your will. You have no choice.*

Jane has labeled what she wants "right" and what he wants "wrong". There's a lot of moral pressure on him: *You've got to pay, John. It's your duty. You're the father. Live up to your obligations. You're not a deadbeat dad, are you?*

John feels stuck. He tries to argue: Of course, he will do what it takes, he wants to be fair. All he wants is to find a way to share responsibilities and expenses. But as soon as he argues against traditional child support – where he has to give Jane money she spends at her discretion - he is called a deadbeat dad. Not just by Jane – by the judge as well.

Arguing doesn't get him anywhere. Words, logic, are powerless. It is depressing: he is bumping his head against the state's law.

moral pressure

They – Jane, the judge – they keep saying: *Pay up!*

John is constantly reminded that what he wants is harmful to "the best interest of the child". He is told that his child needs to be protected from his selfishness. What! He'd tear him away from his own mother! He'd let him starve! Everything that's done to him is done in the name of protecting, so to speak, "the widow and the orphan". Not only is he fighting his wife, he keeps being told he is fighting against his own child.

John knows he is being manipulated. But it's hard for him to resist this manipulation, because he can't bear to be seen as an irresponsible father. He'd like so much for Jane, for the judge, to see things his way, to understand him.

He feels guilty, because he sees that the child is caught in the middle. Jane won't budge, she has the law for her, so it looks to everybody like he is the one making it hard to come to a settlement.

He feels envious of Jane's certainties. She's not hesitating to go all the way to get what she wants. And, the way the system is skewed, she'll win. He hates her for that. And she knows it, she's laughing at his efforts, laughing at him in front of Joey – when she's not depicting him as a selfish creature who's harming his child.

There's no way out of such a prison... he lets the pressure mount... and, finally, there's the emotional outburst: *I'm sick and tired of being pushed around.* John is not actually saying it to anybody. He just lets himself think it: *To hell with you, I have my own needs. I'm tired of just hearing about your needs.*

And there is something very freeing in this anger – at long last, he is in touch with it. He feels lighter. It's like a fog is lifting – everything feels clearer to him.

He now knows: it doesn't have to be that way.

a man's role

It used to be that work was both the burden and the privilege of men. A curse, but also, at least for some of us, an opportunity to achieve a sense of purpose and accomplishment. It used to be that nurturing was both the burden and the privilege of women.

In the past few decades, a lot of attention has been given to going beyond these limited roles. There is now a big emphasis on encouraging men to be more focused on relationships (in particular with our children). In some ways, this is a role reversal from the days when women felt pressure to be more like men – more aggressive, more oriented towards the outside world, career and money. Today, being primarily focused on work is seen as incomplete. Our society's role model is the successful working woman, focused on her work as well as her family – or the man who, like her, balances work and family.

As a result, men are now pulled in two different directions. On the one hand, we are encouraged to be more nurturing. On the other hand, we are still expected to be mostly defined by our work and ability to make money. This reaches a dramatic point in divorce, when fathers are separated from their children and ordered to give the mothers a significant portion of their income as "child support".

Writing a check to the mother is not the same thing as actually buying something for a child, and experiencing the loving feeling it involves. Not only are we deprived of the pleasure of actively nurturing our children... we feel deeply insulted: our ability to love and nurture our children is confined to providing money to their mother. The suffering is material, but, at least as importantly, emotional and spiritual. Each check we write re-opens the wound.

We keep being reminded that, when it comes to parenting, we're not really that important. Worse: We feel like we were set up to compete in a race that was rigged – the adversarial divorce. How could we possibly have hoped to be deemed the equal of a mother in terms of mothering?

We feel betrayed... the same way those women who were prompted to go into the work force as equals felt when they discovered that, deep down, they were considered as outsiders and inferiors in a male world.

they burned bras, we burn wallets

In the sixties and seventies, some women were burning bras to make a statement about liberation. The bra was the symbol of the restraints society placed on women – seeing highly desirable qualities in them, but also limiting them to very specific roles. There's much more than that to a full-fledged human being!

Now, it's our turn to struggle to define our identity, and the meaning of our lives. In fact, the irony is, the pressure we are feeling is similar to what women have been feeling as they have been struggling to go beyond asphyxiating gender roles. The crazy-making ambivalence we experience – be a nurturer *vs.* be a warrior and a money maker – is similar to the crazy-making ambivalence women have been experiencing – be a achiever *vs.* be a Mom and a pretty thing.

The oppressive voice of society used to tell women to stay in their place, to look down on them as harlots when they dared search for their own voice, and, worse, when that voice had the accents of anger.

Now, as men, we keep hearing that being a man means you have to grin and bear it. No, worse, you have to pay. Which ends up being more than just pay for expenses, it ends up sounding like: *You must pay for being a man* – retribution, paying for your original sin of being born a man.

So what are we going to do? Say: *Oh, I'm so sorry, will I ever be able to live it down, to ever atone enough for being a man, to atone for that sin, to repay you for all the suffering that men have inflicted on you women? Yes, I will gladly pay that, and more, too...*

Or: *Hell, no, I won't pay. Not guilty. Get lost!*

In fact, often, we equivocate. We'd like to say: *No, I won't.* But men are not allowed to not want to, so we say: *I can't,* and we get humiliated for it – not man enough to pay, not man enough to make the money they need. And our pleasure at standing up for ourselves is mixed with shame – for not being man enough, for letting them down when they need us.

Women used to burn bras, and they had a lot of fun doing that. In the fire, they were not just burning their bras, they were also burning their guilt. They no longer needed to feel guilty for betraying their sacred duty, as women, to be first and foremost mothers and sex goddesses. They could now go beyond that, be themselves.

There was a wonderful liberating energy in those bonfires, tremendous pleasure in the fight. It is now our turn to carry the torch in the fight for freedom and fulfillment.

the alternative

John is rebelling against the traditional divorce system which says that he must pay the price for divorce – financially as well as emotionally - that it's the only way.

It's not. There is an alternative. It is that the judge steer Jane and John toward cooperation, instead of making the divorce an all-or-nothing fight. How different things would be if the focus of the proceedings was on finding a way to co-parent after divorce!

shared parenting

Shared parenting goes further than what traditional laws call joint custody.

In joint custody (i.e. joint legal custody), both parents have a say in the major decisions of a child's life – e.g. religion, schooling… In practice, the mother usually has physical custody of the child, and the father has very little say over most of what happens in the child's life – among other things, he has to give the mother child support and has no say in how it is spent.

Shared parenting involves both legal and physical custody. There are no pre-set roles where the woman is the nurturer and decision-maker, and the man the money provider. Children may spend equal time with both parents. Regarding money, parents jointly budget for the children's expenses, and each pay equitably for these expenses.

A mother, Merinda M., describes her shared parenting arrangement in the following manner: *I am a sharing parent; my 10 year old son shares equal time with his father as he does with me. We live 2000 miles apart, but the communication is always there. We agreed when we divorced that we would never withhold from our son the time that he would have normally received. It was both of us who created him, and it will be both of us to play an active role in who he becomes.*

how it works

There are no pre-set rules as to how parents have to share parenting responsibilities. While a 50/50 division of time and tasks seems like a reasonable way to start, it could be 90/10 if that is what the parents prefer. The same goes for money –some people may opt to give their ex-spouse a set sum of money every month instead of being involved in the day-to-day decisions of how to use this money for the children (there are even married couples who function this way). The difference is that this is a voluntary choice, not something dictated by gender roles.

Several states have now adopted laws which call for a presumptive shared parenting; little by little, more will undoubtedly follow. The presumption means that shared parenting is expected to continue after divorce.

Of course, these laws make allowances for cases where one parent is unfit, and it is better for the child to remain in sole custody of the other parent. So what's the difference between laws that have a presumption of shared parenting and traditional laws?

With the traditional laws, unless both parents agree to share parenting, the courts undertake an inquiry as to the better parent. As we have seen, this usually means that father is eliminated and the mother is selected as the parent in charge.

With a presumption of shared parenting, it is not possible for either parent to deny shared parenting without grounds. When a father wants to stay actively involved in his child's life, he doesn't have to prove that they he is *more fit* to be a parent than the mother. There is no need to argue whether or not a man can be as nurturing as a woman.

If the mother does not want shared parenting, she has to prove that the father is actually unfit (instead of just relying on the perception that, if the court has to choose one parent, the mother is the natural choice).

why it's good for men

There is a lot to be gained for men in leaving the adversarial game.

After all, this game is predicated on finding the better parent – which, essentially, means something like: finding the parent who is most like our ideal image of what a mother is. In most cases, a man just can't prove to judges that he is more of a mother than his ex-wife is. Because he's not a mother, he's not a woman.

You're in a game that is rigged against you when the rules are defined that way. By definition, you can rarely win. You mostly have a chance to humiliate yourself.

The truth is: You're not a mother. You're a father. You're still a parent. And your child deserves two parents.

why it's good for children

Children indeed want to keep both parents. Writes Charles of his 3-year old daughter:

She loves us both and is very sensitive. She knows when we have a problem between us. She takes her mother's hands and my hands and puts them together, or takes her mother's face and my face and puts them together, or else she takes one of our hands and she holds the other hand and she is in between.

Presiding Judge Dorothy T. Beasley, of the Georgia Court of Appeals, wrote a very moving statement of a child's right to shared parenting[5]:

Although the dispute is symbolized by a 'versus' which signi-

*fies two adverse parties at opposite poles of a line, there is in fact
a third party whose interests and rights make of the line a tri-
angle. That person, the child who is not an official party to the
lawsuit but whose well-being is in the eye of the controversy, has
a right to shared parenting when both are equally suited to provide it. Inherent in the express public policy is a recognition of
the child's right to equal access and opportunity with both parents, the right to be guided and nurtured by both parents, the
right to have major decisions made by the application of both
parents' wisdom, judgement and experience. The child does not
forfeit these rights when the parents divorce.*

why it's good for women

Quite a few women and women's groups fight shared parenting in the name of feminism. They are very vocal about it
and, as a result, there is a widespread perception that shared
parenting is a code word for harming mothers and *their (!)*
children.

It is true that shared parenting sharply curtails the two
major advantages that mothers enjoy within the traditional
divorce system.

If mothers are no longer almost automatically awarded
custody, they can no longer refuse to cooperate with the
fathers in co-parenting; and they can no longer leverage this
to threaten fathers and get better terms in discussing other
issues in the divorce settlement.

Financially, shared parenting implies that the parents find
an equitable way to each contribute to the children's expens-

es. The mothers then lose the total control they traditionally have over how the child support money is used; additionally, they may receive less money than they traditionally have – especially when the father is actively involved in parenting and incurs expenses.

So it is understandable that many women would feel threatened by a change in which they have something to lose. But women also have much to gain as well from shared parenting - this is why prominent feminists like Karen DeCrow, a former president of NOW, favor shared parenting. With the father more involved in the children's lives, divorced women have less tension and more freedom to pursue outside interests – including new relationships. The loss of the traditional advantage is the price to pay for equality and new opportunities.

After all, this is only the logical continuation of the long-standing plea from women that men be more involved in the children's care. As Supreme Court Justice Ruth Ginsburg so eloquently stated, *When fathers take equal responsibility for the care of their children, that's when women will be truly liberated.* [6]

is it a panacea?

The frequency of shared parenting has steadily grown. It was almost unheard of before 1970, and it now accounts for more than one out of five divorces[7].

Does it always work - for every couple? No, not any more than any other solution to human problems is 100% perfect for all situations and all people. But, on the whole, studies

show shared parenting to be work much better than the traditional divorce. Time and again, it has been demonstrated
that children do better with both parents active in their lives
after divorce (see the report of the U.S. Commission on
Child and Family Welfare in the appendix).

And money problems – which the traditional system uses
as the justification for its tactics – are actually much fewer
with shared parenting. Government statistics[8] show that:
- 44.5% of fathers with no visitation pay the support due
- 79.1% of fathers with visitation privileges pay the support
  due
- 90.2% of fathers with joint custody pay the support due

Do shared parenting laws mean the end of problems for
fathers? No, even in states like California, which have had a
presumption of shared parenting for years, there are still dis-
gruntled fathers. But, let's look at it this way. It has been
decades since the beginning of the Civil Rights movement,
and we're still not a color-blind society. Is this a reason to say
we shouldn't have taken the steps we took to improve the situation?

What does this mean to John – and to divorced fathers in
general?

On a social level, it means that we owe it to ourselves, to
other parents, and to our children, to fight for changing
divorce laws when they don't have a provision for shared parenting.

On a personal level, it is reassuring to see that shared parenting enjoys widespread support and is a growing trend.

We're not as alone as we may feel when we are rebuked by our ex, by a judge, by the laws of our state. We certainly are not out of our minds for wanting to share parenting – it may actually be the opposite that's true.

equality vs.
one up /one down

The traditional divorce system seems to work to Jane's advantage, in the sense that she is getting her way. But it is truly demeaning to both John and Jane – and damaging to their child.

Each parent is encouraged to prove how bad the other one is. And this is horrible, inhuman. A real human being doesn't need to be perfect to have the right to live his life, or to have the right to be a parent to his child. Only in adversarial divorces does it come to feel that way.

With mediation, the power to make decisions is kept inside the family system instead of being assumed by an outsider.

What gives the judge the authority to determine who the better parent is? What does he actually know about parenting, about what's good for children? Would any sane people turn to a judge to ask him how to raise their kids?

The quarrel between John and Jane has created a vacuum – which the judge is willing to fill. He sees his task as selecting the better parent. This may seem normal – simply because this is what most judges have been doing. But this is not the only way to solve the conflict – in fact, as we have seen before, shared parenting would work better.

So why is the judge doing this?

conflict resolution

The judge's basic assumption is that parents who disagree will not be able to effectively co-parent, that they will continue to fight with each other in a way that will be harmful to the children.

His solution is to attempt to eliminate conflict by effectively giving all parental authority to one parent. This seems to echo the wisdom of Solomon's judgment – you can't divide a child between two would-be parents without killing the child.

Now, this seems normal – which means there is the weight of tradition, of habits, behind this way of thinking. We are so accustomed to it that it seems to be an obvious truth, instead of realizing it is just an assumption, a way of seeing the world – not a universal truth.

For one thing, while the adversarial process is often seen

as a normal way to deal with divorce, it certainly is not the only method society uses to solve problems. And fortunately so.

Where would we be as a civilization, if we believed that the only way to resolve disagreements is to have one winner and one loser? The progress of civilization has been to replace the law of the jungle with rules that curb our tendency to deal with conflict by trying to eliminate the opponent.

We approve of competition in business, but we tame capitalism in the name of social responsibility. We have antitrust laws to curb predatory practices. We may argue about how much of a safety net society should provide for the neediest, but the concept of having some form of a safety net is generally accepted. Even in war, we believe that there are limits that should not be transgressed – otherwise, we call what happens "war crimes". So why should we rely on the law of the jungle for conflict resolution in divorce?

different conceptions of the family

There are profound philosophical differences between the traditional laws and shared parenting in terms of what it is to be a family.

The traditional laws see divorce as breaking the family unit; after the break-up, assets as well as responsibilities are divided so as to separate the two parties as much as possible.

With the spread of divorce, many people have adopted more fluid concepts of what constitutes a family, and these concepts are reflected in the shared parenting approach to divorce. Essentially, the parents' function of raising a child together continues after they are separated.

The parents are now leading separate lives (they may in fact now be married to other partners, and even have other children in these marriages)... but they continue to assume the function of the original family, which is to raise the child they made together. This is what family therapist Constance Ahrons calls the bi-nuclear family.

There's a state of flow, where several families co-exist. In order for a new family to be created, the old one doesn't need to be annihilated.

peer vs. abusive relationships

Shared parenting fosters a relationship of peers – it is based on mutual respect, on respect for differences of opinion, and a common desire to overcome emotional difficulties in order to be good parents. The parents learn that they can disagree yet be able to work out a compromise. The children have a model of how to develop better patterns of communication and problem-solving – ultimately, how to create emotionally-attuned intimate relationships.

This is in sharp contrast what happens in adversarial divorces. The court trains people to be adversaries, whereas mediation trains people to focus on what they have in common – the welfare of their children – and to find ways to effectively co-parent.

The traditional laws all-too-often function like a presumption of custody by the mother. This creates a power imbalance, a one-up/one-down relationship between the parents, that fosters an on-going climate of distrust, insecurity and power plays.

The following chart[9] was originally created to describe
the differences between a healthy relationship and one in
which the woman was abused. It is striking how well it works
in describing the differences between shared parenting and
the adversarial divorce. No wonder: the one up/one down
relationship is fundamentally abusive.

Equality	*Power and control*
Shared responsibility	*One person up / one down*
Economic partnership	*Economic leverage*
Negotiation and fairness	*Coercion and threats*
Respect and trust	*Emotional and/or sexual abuse*
Non-threatening behavior	*Intimidation and / or physical abuse*
Accountability and honesty	*Minimization, denial, blame*
Support and outside connections	*Isolation*
Responsible parenting	*Exploiting children*

abuse and violence

In her court papers, Jane claims that John is abusive, that he is dangerous – to her and to their child. Jane's lawyer suggested these lines – she said it puts Jane in a sympathetic light, it's the normal thing to do. These allegations are not substantiated by any specifics, so the judge doesn't pay much attention to them. And yet, their very presence is upsetting to John.

Maybe it's something about *where there's smoke, there's fire* – even unsubstantiated, the allegations sully him. Maybe he also perceives his vulnerability: what if Jane decided to go all out, to make up stronger accusations? Then, how easy would it be for him to prove his innocence? It would essentially be his word against hers.

ambiguity

Even in cases where violence does occur, there can be some ambiguity as to what really happens. Take Clark's story:

As a result of finally snapping and saying the wrong things after ten years of such insult, negation, humiliation, and far more I was taken in handcuffs from my home, left in a jail for 4 days, and then thrown out on the streets penniless. She had emptied all accounts, had me barred from any communication and from the home.

I have lost access to any of my personal possessions, my assets, my home, and now stand to lose everything personally and professionally in divorce and criminal charges thanks to a hearing in which she and my son crucified me, and a police report in which she added even more horrible lies.

There is no excuse for Clark's "snapping". In doing it, he is descending into the abyss – resorting to violence, by itself, *is* the abyss.

But, while physical violence is terrifying and totally objectionable, it is also terrifying to live in a word where false or exaggerated allegations that can so easily sink a man are so easy to make.

true or false

How is it determined whether an accusation is true or false when there is no conclusive evidence? This is where judgments, arbitrary decisions are made. And errors are made, one way or the other.

After decades of ignoring domestic violence, judges have become more aware of it in recent years. They have come to know that, very often, there is no conclusive proof that domestic violence occurred, even when it did. So, where many judges would previously err in not believing the accuser's claim, many now err in giving her the benefit of the doubt.

One can understand why some judges would want to err on the side of protecting the women: domestic violence against women is a horrible thing – not just for what it does to the women, but also for the impact it has on children.

And yet, many people – not just women – believe that too many cases of violence go unpunished. The most spectacular "proof" of their claim was the OJ Simpson verdict, where the man seemed to literally get away with murder .

It is impossible for a society to be totally fair to everybody. Choices have to be made. As an individual judge, but also as a society, we make choices. This is a social contract, where the line is drawn in such a way as to reflect our values - and the respective powers of the groups in presence.

If one places a priority on protecting the innocent from being unfairly punished, one uses only the most stringent criteria to define who is guilty. It is then quite conceivable that many perpetrators will get away with it (including, probably, some of the most wicked ones).

On the other hand, if one wants to punish every possible perpetrator, even when the evidence is not incontrovertible, then many innocents will be punished for crimes they didn't commit.

the abusive context

I would like to suggest that the problem of abuse in divorce is not limited to those cases where there is actual physical abuse. I also consider as highly abusive those situations where the mother makes false claims of physical abuse in order to gain tactical advantage over her husband – this may not be physical abuse, but it is very potent emotional abuse.

But I wouldn't even limit the definition of abuse in divorce to these cases. I believe the whole situation of the traditional, adversarial divorce is a context that fosters abusive attitudes and behaviors on both sides. Sometimes, this gets acted out in physical violence – and it's not always violence of the man against the woman (see notes) – but the abuse is more pervasive than that.

Even when there is no physical violence, the adversarial system fosters a climate of all-out war in which the end justifies the means. The parties become obsessed with destroying each other emotionally. The battle is conducted in the name of the children, yet the children, who are in the middle of all this turmoil and feel somehow responsible for it, are probably the most deeply abused parties.

There's a lot of talk about preventing violence. Something should be done to curb the mechanism that fans the flames – the adversarial process itself.

the longing

John has been reading a lot and thinking a lot about how to deal with divorce, what makes sense for the children. He believes what he wants is reasonable – that shared parenting is not just good for himself, but for his child as well, and, actually, for Jane too. How can Jane not see it? How can the judge not see it? How can the laws not see it?

There's a longing in him – that the judge, or some benevolent authority, will stand up to tell Jane: *I understand you don't want to have to deal with John, that you'd rather be the child's parent without him... But this is too damaging to the child. We just can't let you have your way here.*

It would be so nice if what happens in fairy tales always

happened in real life – that the righteous always prevails, even if only at the eleventh hour.

But what happens is that the judge sides with Jane and admonishes John, telling him, in effect, to go away.

John's dilemma is a tough one. Jane and the judge are telling him to admit he's wrong, to let go of his desire to remain the involved father he'd like to be, to give his wife control of the child-support money, and to get on with his life. If he does that, he feels he's betraying himself and letting down his child.

The alternative doesn't seem very bright either. John feels like he's banging his head against a wall. He could be spending the rest of his life in a exile of his own making, muttering to himself: *I was right, I am right, and they're all wrong.*

he is right...
but he can't have what he wants

They win – Jane, the powers-that-be. It doesn't mean John is wrong. When slavery was the norm, it was not wrong to be an abolitionist. When segregation was the law, it was not wrong to fight for desegregation…

So, John may be right… but he can't have what he wants.

John feels trampled, humiliated by Jane, by the judge... He has an almost tactile sensation of the raw power of the system - the callousness with which it is treating him.

He is choked up by conflicting emotions. It would be so tempting to stomp his foot on the ground, to cry: *it's unfair, unfair, unfair!* His eyes well up with tears, his heart is so heavy it's about to burst. But he can't cry - what's the point?

It's going to be even worse for him if he cries. They'll make fun of him for being so childish. He feels all alone, against a hostile world where anything he does will be misunderstood. It's his lot to be the victim who appears to all the world to be the culprit.

It's so unfair! How dare they!

After the outrage comes the frustration, then the anger – sharp like a sword that would destroy all that is in the way. From the anger comes the energy that helps fight – not just through the legal battles, but also the emotional obstacles that get in the way of his getting what he wants out of life.

And, below the anger, the deep, gnawing pain. From the pain will come the softness that allows him to be more in touch with his inner self, more compassionate with himself and others – and more able to feel emotionally close to his child.

**part three:
resolve & wisdom**

It takes a spirited fight for John to overcome all the obstacles that stand in the way of his staying involved in his child's life.

There are ups and downs – and it often feels like there are more downs than ups. It's not easy to keep the spirit when the whole situation seems like a huge mess, when everything and everybody seems to turn against you.

How do you keep the spirit then? When you feel overwhelmed by the pressure, consumed by anger, fear and self-doubt?

To successfully stave off all the outside pressures, you need the inner strength that comes from being comfortable with who you are and what you want. The strength of your conviction comes from a solid sense of your inner truth – in contrast to the brittleness of rigid dogma, protective armor, defensive arguments… And this conviction, this sense of inner peace, comes from confronting your inner fears.

Looking inside is not a substitute for action – it happens in parallel, as we are trying to make sense of all the crazy, terrifying nonsense that we are trying our best to deal with. Adversity is a powerful incentive to reflect on who we are, deep down. To find personal meaning and spiritual connection, and the strength that comes from knowing our personal truth.

The more comfortable you are with yourself, the more you like yourself, the better influence you'll be on your child. You need to trust your own power as a human being, to feel it from inside.

The stronger you are emotionally, the better you'll be able to cope with this and other big losses – you won't be as overwhelmed by them.

When the roof collapses, you build another roof. Fight back – not necessarily in the sense of getting embroiled in everlasting court battles. Rebuild your life – for yourself, and for your child. This struggle is about regaining your inner power. In addition to fighting with your ex and with the legal system, you're also fighting a battle within yourself - coming to grips with just how long to keep fighting, what to keep fighting for, and how.

The opposite of despair is faith. This is about finding a way to regain faith that, somehow, life can be good after all. That you have a place in the world, and that you can protect it.

It's not about putting on a mask of fake optimism, fake cheerfulness. It's about embarking on a journey to find in yourself the ability to regain hope in life.

You owe it to your child to get a life.

like facing death

John is standing in front of the judge. He's a grown-up man - a father. Yet, he looks like a little boy caught doing something wrong. A little boy, head down, humiliated. He's had to stand there, silent, hearing all this abuse hurled at him. It wasn't called abuse, it was called advice – the judge telling him how to behave as a responsible man, a man who cares for his child.

what it feels like

John is in pain, he can't stand it. He'd like to run, to scream. He has to stay still, knowing he's going to get whipped. The end is near, unavoidable. He doesn't have a prayer. Why is he fighting, why is he resisting? He doesn't have a chance. There's no way he can win. Why doesn't he just accept what's going to happen anyway? What's the point of fighting? Superior force is closing in on him. He's about to be destroyed.

It feels like it's *them* against him – Jane, the judge, the court, all of society – ganging up against him to crush him.

John feels like he's facing a humongous crawling-chaos of a monster. How can he possibly approach it? The Monster has a way of winning through intimidation. Moving so many heads, so fast, that it seems to create an impenetrable barricade. *Don't even try!* hisses the Monster. *You don't stand a chance. You don't even know where to begin.*

If John succeeds in cutting off one of its heads, another one turns at him, hissing, spitting venom, ready to bite and kill, made even more furious by his successful attack: *How dare you fight me?* The monster is going to kill him, and he brought it all on himself. What business did he have to awaken the beast?

surrender

They keep telling him to surrender. *They?* Jane, the judge, and well-wishers who claim to only have his own good in mind, who tell him that surrender is the way to true freedom. It doesn't matter who; at this point, it all seems to be coming from the same voice, the voice of the Monster hellbent on destroying him.

So John resists: *All you want is to gain control of me. To turn me into a zombie.*

It's for your own good, they say as they try to muzzle him. And he's supposed to accept it, to let go. They tell him not to be so uptight, so old fashioned, so hung up; that "surrender" doesn't mean he's losing. Far from that, they say, surrender means going with the flow, accepting the inevitable, becoming one with the universe. Cosmic consciousness, spirituality… instead of the misguided macho sense of honor that makes him refuse to accept the inevitable. *Hey, it's no defeat, it's for the benefit of your child. And you'll come to see it's also for your own good.*

John is outraged: *How can you tell me with a straight face that surrender is good for me? Only in the sense that you're ready to crush me if I move any more.*

Trust me, they say. *Once you surrender, you'll see things differently. All resistance is futile, useless. When are you going to get it? Stop this childish nonsense.*

fear of annihilation

Clearly, John is afraid that he'll be vanquished, humiliated, annihilated by the what he sees as the superior forces of Jane, the judge, the laws… ganging up against him.

But there's another fear of annihilation as well. The fear that, in some way, he might betray himself - lose himself - if he starts to see the situation differently.

There's a difference between both.

In the first case, John's fear is about an *external* source – what he sees as the juggernaut of Jane's will and the pressure from the judge, the court, and society in general that he cave in. This is an adversarial situation, in which one party has to lose so that the other may win. Fear is legitimate.

The other fear of annihilation is about *internal* processes. It is the fear that an old self must die before a new self is born. A new self? That is, a new way of seeing reality. As we confront difficult situations, we learn that some of our ways of dealing with the world hamper us more than they help us. We progressively let go of them, as we acquire new perspectives. This is a scary process, akin to the death of an old self – a mentor that we trusted for so many years that we find it hard to imagine living without it.

on death and dying

In her book "On Death and Dying", Elisabeth Kübler-Ross[10] described a type of emotional journey among people who are facing death. Since she wrote this book, the model has been found to apply as well, for many people, to other major losses.

Typically, the first reaction to news of impending doom is <u>denial</u> – *it's not true, it can't possibly happen to me, there must be a mistake.* John doesn't quite believe that a nasty divorce can happen to him, so to speak – it only happens to others, doesn't it? That Jane would drag him to court to have her way, to take everything she can from him as if he were an enemy. He can't quite believe that, to her, he is the enemy. Even though he's beginning to hate her.

Elisabeth Kübler-Ross observed that facing the reality of death leads people to feel very <u>angry</u>, resentful, rageful. *This is so unfair!*, says our hero, John – and this is when he's at his most restrained. He's angry at Jane, but also at the court, the laws, the "system"… It's unfair that, in this conflict situation he's in, the other party has the upper hand.

What do people do when they keep bumping their heads against the seeming invincibility of their opponent? This is the time for <u>unrealistic bargaining</u> – *I'll give you this, and you'll give me what I want.* There's nothing wrong about bargaining – when it is based on offering the other party something they might really be interested in. John keeps offering what he believes Jane should want – but why should she accept to share equitably with him, when she doesn't have to? This bargaining is still a way of not dealing with the real balance of power in the situation.

Once the reality of death sets in, the patients feel overwhelmed, they become <u>depressed</u>. *All resistance is futile.* And, indeed, John has often been wondering whether there is any point at all to fighting.

Anger, unrealistic bargaining, depression… this is our struggle against "real" problems in the outside world, but also against our own inner demons.

Some dying people eventually reach a stage where they are fully aware of impending death, and neither angry nor depressed about it. They <u>accept</u> it.

acceptance

For a divorced father, acceptance of reality need not be synonymous with capitulation, humiliating defeat.

We may have to accept that the situation makes it difficult, or even impossible, to be the fathers we want to be. But we don't have to give up our right to be an involved parent.

There is a difference between accepting what is inescapable – like death, when you're dying – and cowardly surrendering when you could have fought more. And acceptance need not mean losing your integrity – it can sometimes be quite the opposite.

Acceptance is not betrayal.

Acceptance is about using the lessons we learned in life to come to terms with the realities of the world, on our own terms.

we all need support

John feels all alone – he's not just fighting against Jane, he feels the judge and the legal system are against him, and he feels misunderstood and criticized by society at large.

He feels threatened, attacked from all sides. So he clams up, he closes up his armor. The relaxed smile of happy times is replaced by a tight face. There's tension in his shoulders, in the back of his neck, in his frown… There's contraction and constriction everywhere – the opposite of the sense of openness and the radiant smile that come from feeling safe and secure. He is clamping down, trying to regroup behind his shield.

It's all well and good, inasmuch as being closed up this

way protects him from the "enemy". But, unfortunately, it
also isolates him from other people as well. This protective
shield stays sealed even in places where he doesn't need it –
where he would, in fact, benefit from being more open. It
prevents him from opening up, from finding mutual support
in contact with others who are in similar situations.

alone in the world

Divorced fathers often have a sense of being alone in the
world. We're told that we are not as deserving as our wives.
Told not only that our needs don't count, but also that they
are harmful to our children. Each of us is treated as if he were
the bad guy. We don't have a strong sense of belonging to a
segment of society that shares common interests.

When discontent is organized into a movement – as it
was for Blacks, or for feminists - there is a sense of "us" vs.
"them". As a Black person, or as a woman, you belong to a
visible subgroup of society - it's not one individual against
the world, it's one subgroup against another. The subgroups
have developed words for the "other" ("The White Man"…
"Male Chauvinist Pig"…).

When there is no organized movement, each individual
father is isolated against not just his wife, his judge, but also
the whole of society (witness how uninhibited society is in
indulging in "deadbeat dad bashing").

Divorced fathers don't have the support of a highly visible organized movement to help define themselves as an

integral part of society. We experience our struggle as that of an individual against society – the struggle of the powerless against the all-powerful.

This is akin to the struggle a little child may have with all-powerful parents who are not attuned to his needs. This child's struggle is: *how can I ask for what I want, and still be accepted?* The less understanding the parents are, the harder it is for the child to develop into a strong individual.

divorced dads, unite

We don't have to do it alone. Actually, we'll do much better if we're not alone. Where else can we find acceptance if not among our peers?

If you're reading this book, you're on the right track. The first step is to get a sense that you're not alone. What is happening to you has also been happening to millions of other fathers.

What happened to each of us individually may have made us feel shell-shocked… Well, it is time for us to come out of our shells, to connect with others, and to speak out. If we don't claim a better world for ourselves and our children, who else will?

The next step is to actively seek contact with others.

There's some truth to the cliché: *Men don't ask for help.* We're conditioned to grin and bear it. We don't know how to admit defeat and powerlessness. It looks too much like being a loser, it looks so unmanly, even to those of us who are not into macho strutting.

We want to live up to the image society has of men, so we don't admit how powerless we feel. As if this were not enough, we also get clobbered – by women, by the courts - for looking so powerful.

It is difficult for us to join – or even find – a group. This is part of the struggle, and part of the solution.

what to do in a group

Just being part of a group of like-minded people is a great first step. It's a great way to pool concrete information about how the system works. And there's a wonderful therapeutic effect in hearing the stories of other men. For one thing, you clearly see that you're not alone. You get a sense of community – this is a powerful antidote to the sense that society undervalues you.

Groups function in many different ways. Some groups focus on specific tasks (for instance, people who represent themselves in court - *pro se* legal defense; informing the media, monitoring the courts…) while others are more geared to providing emotional support.

If you're starting a group, a good way to break the ice is to start as a discussion group. Select a relevant book – for instance this one. Assign a chapter for each meeting. The meeting consists in each member bringing up their personal experiences around the topic of the chapter. I mean, really personal experiences, as opposed to generalities, or stylistic comments - this is about getting personal.

you can solve your own problems
by helping others to solve theirs

In a support group, you form strong bonds of trust with fellow men. You find a place to express your rage and your pain confidentially, in the company of sympathetic men.

Of course, the purpose is not to stay in rage and pain, but to express these feelings in order to go beyond them. The point is, you have to start by having a place where the anger is accepted, and where the pain is met with compassion. Therapy allows you to do that in much more depth than a peer support group. It is likely to bring out the complexities underlying your life – what happened between you and your ex, what behaviors you exhibit in all areas of your life… It helps uncover the conscious and unconscious models you have formed of what it is to be a man.

But a support group is not just a cheap substitute for therapy. It is a way of helping yourself by helping others.

Over time, you get some perspective on your situation. On the one hand, you see there are tremendous similarities between you and the other fathers. On the other hand, you also notice tremendous differences between individual situations. You feel compassion for other people's struggles and pain; you also feel that these people can understand you.

Jim Cook, founder of the Joint Custody Association, and a prime mover behind many states' efforts to enact laws that have a presumption of joint custody/shared parenting, has this advice for fathers: "A good recipe for overcoming depression is to tell yourself that, for every moment of anxiety and frustration, you're going to put in an equal amount of time and energy as an activist to promote change."

how to find a group

It's not that easy to find or form a group, but it can be done if you put some time and effort into it. Here are a few suggestions.

Look around for local support groups. You're more likely to find a workshop or an on-going group for divorced people (men and women) than one especially geared to fathers. Look for this at local churches, temples, YMCA's, and adult education centers.

Check out the Resources listings at the end of this book for national organizations. Contact them to find the local chapter that's closest to you.

If there is no such group where you live, why not start one? Put out notices on bulletin boards (YMCA, bookstores, libraries, Courthouse...) and local newspapers. Contact the national organizations (e.g. CRC) to see if they have names of other people in your area who may be interested in starting a local group. This is exactly how, several years ago, we started the New York City chapter of CRC.

spreading the word

Powerlessness is feeling there's nobody to hear us, nobody who cares. One way to fight it is to initiate the caring ourselves. If nobody comes to us, we go out and spread the word. We start talking to fellow divorced dads. We write to the media and to politicians. This is how vocal minorities function: their voice is amplified because most people are silent. Men are far too silent. It's time to correct the imbalance.

It felt so good, so liberating, to spread the word. We feel grateful for what validation we have received, so we help others. They appreciate it and they thank us – we experience ourselves as helpful, giving, nurturing. We're good people.

victim no more

When John talks about his situation as a divorced father, the word that seems to come out most often to his lips is "unfair". He feels victimized by Jane, by the courts, by the system. What's adding insult to injury, is that he doesn't feel *seen* for who he is - a loving father, a decent human being. He feels that the court and society treat him as somebody who wouldn't do the right thing by his children if he were not coerced into it - a bogeyman figure with no relationship to who he really is.

the dance of shame and the shadow

There's a "dance" that takes place within each of us individually, as well as at the level of society as a whole. The "dance" we have with the Shadow – the side of us that we don't like to see and we'd rather disown.

Individually, we do not feel that we are dealing with *our* Shadow. Our experience is actually that we find ourselves reluctantly cast into personifying the "Shadow" side of society: we are excluded – deemed no longer fit to be "real" parents. Most of our moves are ascribed to selfish motives that are against the interest of our children. We are on a slippery slope. The more hurt we feel, the more we squirm to get out of that awful situation, the more misunderstood we are – and the worse we look to the rest of society. It keeps going from bad to worse – it can go to the extreme of being rejected, reviled deadbeat dads, jailed dads.

We feel the despair of seeing ourselves reflected in the eyes of the "good people" as the feared and despised Shadow. As we suffer from this situation, it is understandable that we'd want to find ways to bridge the gap between us and the rest of society, to increase communication and understanding instead of hostility. There's a deep longing: *If only they could see us for who we really are…*

There is indeed value in fostering better communication. But only trying to convince *them* to better listen does not address the deep wound of the Shadow within ourselves. To elaborate on this, I find it useful to use the metaphor of the alcoholic.

the alcoholic as a metaphor

In practical terms, there is a world of difference between

alcoholics and "normal" people. So much so that "normal" people and alcoholics themselves consider alcoholism a disease - sometimes with a medical connotation, and sometimes with a moral connotation (as in "this is sick").

This way of seeing things seems natural and objective. Yet it has hidden costs. What happens is that we are splitting the world into a dichotomy - normal and abnormal, healthy and sick, good and bad. When we do this, we conveniently avoid seeing that there is a Shadow side in all of us. We don't like to see this side, we do our best not to see it. But it exists, and it finds ways to show up. Instead of all of us owning up to both our bright side and our dark side, we end up having a division of labor of sorts. Most people try their best to hide the Shadow side as completely as possible, to be "normal". And some people "volunteer", so to speak, to act out the Shadow side for all of society.

The "good" side of our society is that part of us that values restraint, reason, a sense of purpose. The Alcoholic, on the other hand, represents that part of us that feels despair and lets go of restraint. I mean, we're not all alcoholics, but we all have in us a part that feels despair. This part is acted out by the alcoholic.

Within any and all of us, there are both sides. Just like a child of divorce feels torn between Mom and Dad, our task is to experience this feeling of being torn within ourselves, and to find a way of being whole.

dancing with our shadow

It is said that, even deep in his grave, Cain would hear

God asking him: Why did you kill your brother Abel? At some point, we realize we cannot run far enough to escape the relentless taunting of the "Good" – because that voice, too, is within ourselves. Not only are we the Shadow, we are also the voice of the "Good" lashing out at this Shadow in us.

The first step of the Alcoholic's recovery is to admit he's an alcoholic. He stands up, and says: *Yes, I am the Shadow.* In so doing, he no longer is the shadow, *and* he no longer is the outraged voice of the Righteous cursing the Shadow. This is the beginning of his journey of self-discovery.

Strangely enough, only the first Step of Alcoholics Anonymous says something about the struggle with alcohol. The other Steps provide a framework to, essentially, "get a life". One of the key insights of AA is that the best way to abandon destructive habits is to have something better to look forward to.

The roadmap that AA gives the alcoholic has nothing to do with getting society to show more tolerance toward him. It is about getting the alcoholic to find *acceptance* of his own limitations, so that he can deal with them realistically.

For divorced fathers as well as for any people that find themselves cast in the role of the Shadow, the beginning of sanity is to recognize how we are internally buying into this role, and to explore how much more there is to us than that.

facing the truth

When the recovering alcoholic admits to being powerless, it's not towards blaming what he drinks, or other people, or society at large. He's just noticing what is happening to him. The Alcoholic is not glorifying his powerlessness. He is facing it. In everyday language, we call this a sobering thought. How appropriate! The very fact of facing the reality of alcoholism is sobering.

What's liberating for the alcoholic is to admit his lack of control in an area where it had been important for him to claim power. He used to think he could control his drinking. That he could stop drinking any time he really wanted to… so that, meanwhile, he could have another glass, and yet another… He could handle it…

Admitting powerlessness is how the alcoholic starts to take responsibility for his actions: once he admits he can't control alcohol, he has to stop drinking.

In other words, the road to sanity for the alcoholic is not the kind of powerlessness that makes him roll into the gutter after he's drunk. Losing his shirt is not what necessarily cures the gambler. It may help, in the sense that the shock compels him to face reality, and to start bottoming out. But there is nothing inherently therapeutic about rolling into the gutter, or losing one's shirt.

The alcoholic's First Step to sanity is to literally speak the truth, to describe reality as simply and directly as possible: *Alcohol doesn't work for me, and yet I keep doing it. In fact, when I use it, things end up being worse.*

Before this, the alcoholic is either in denial (*I can deal with it*) or so overwhelmed that he's given up (*What's the point of even trying?*). He's in an all-or-nothing situation. The reality is that, while this drinking problem is difficult to control, it can be controlled, one day at a time.

When he acknowledges he's powerless over alcohol, the alcoholic puts his efforts where he has some power – in his own actions. What he chooses to deal with, day in and day out, is stopping to drink – as opposed to getting overwhelmed by feeling powerless over alcohol.

For John, empowerment lies in finding a way to speak the truth of his situation – what he's powerless about, and what he can act on.

He's powerless over a lot of what's happening in his divorce. In particular, he's powerless over what Jane does or doesn't do. He can't control her. And he's powerless over the laws and custom of divorce (even if he fights to change them, they won't apply retroactively). He has to avoid the temptation to use the language of powerlessness to avoid responsibility for his actions – i.e. "they" took power from him, implying "they" have to restore power to him.

something is changing

In the court room, John feels he is at the mercy of the judge; who feels he is protecting the woman; who feels she needs it *because she's weaker and vulnerable to the man.*

Men feel powerless over women, who derive their power from their powerlessness over men.

The temptation is strong for John to do as Jane does – to complain about his powerlessness, about being victimized. And why not? Isn't it the way it seems to work? Isn't it the reason everything is done to "protect" Jane?

But all he'd accomplish this way is continuing the vicious cycle of using powerlessness as a way to gain power. And what good has this been doing him?

powerlessness

How does John experience his powerlessness?

John asks for shared parenting. Jane refuses. She says: *things will happen my way.*

At this moment, he sees her as all-powerful. And he collapses. He thinks: *This is the beginning of the end. She'll win. I don't have a leg to stand on.* And he doesn't stand on his own two feet. He's in a fog. He's like an insect glued to the spider's web, paralyzed, waiting to be devoured. The more he moves, the more entangled he becomes. All resistance is futile. It feels so true, because it echoes deep fears. *You don't have a right to it. You must pay, be punished. You knew it all along, you thought you might have been able to escape your fate, but you really can't.* It's like an orgy of powerlessness.

It's an exceptionally unpleasant experience - feeling out of control in a scary, hostile environment. John feels humiliated – his own will is trampled by Jane's and the court's. He is also in a lot of fear – where is it all going?

Yet, at the same time, there is an odd kind of pleasure in resisting what Jane wants, an odd sense of power in the powerlessness... *Your victory will not be complete, because I will not be a willing part to it. You have to drag me through it, kicking and screaming.*

There's also an odd kind of reassurance. John feels he doesn't have any responsibility for what happens. She's in charge, so it's all *her* fault. In a way, the worst things get, the more vindicated John can feel. The more the child suffers, the more it "proves" that John was right, and Jane was wrong.

responsibility

Emotionally, it's an understandable reaction. John is in a lot of pain – the loss of a normal relationship with his child, the humiliation in the battle of wills with Jane. This pain is so strong that he feels: *If I can't be part of his life, he might as well be unhappy. In fact, I'd rather he be unhappy – it will show her* (Jane), *it will show them* (the court, society, whoever is preventing him from being an involved father).

But this reaction is not one that John really wants to act on. In fact, a shift occurs in him when he realizes the absurdity and horror of the *victimized* position - he has to hope that his child will suffer in order to be proven right. This is the ultimate no-win situation.

As Joey's father, he does want his child's happiness, even if he's not a part of it.

John's heart opens up when he sees how much he's willing to give his child, without anything in return.

His life begins to change.

He begins to notice how he has been caught up in the adversarial battle – seeing things from the perspective of a battle of wills, of power and control.

control

It has been very painful for John to face how little influence – let alone control - he has over his family. From being an equally important parent during marriage, he's suddenly becoming superfluous - or so it would seem society thinks. From having an equal say over decisions concerning his child, he's left on the sidelines.

John has been feeling that Jane is the control freak in the family – wanting to control him, Joey, everything. But... even to the extent that John's simply trying to reduce the damage she's causing, he's trying to control her. *Damage control is still control.*

John wants to believe he can control Jane (even though he can't). When he believes this, he gets into even more despair. Because he keeps banging his head against the wall that separates what he'd like the world to be, and the reality that is.

It's difficult for John to let go of the illusion that he could be in control. Like a little child who believes that, if he decided to, he'd only have to flap his arms and he'd fly like a bird.

We are what we are, not what we think we should be.

In this sense, John's problem is very similar to that of the alcoholic: It's so important for the alcoholic to believe he has power over alcohol that he can't see his lack of power over it. He just keeps seeing excuses that "explain" why he got drunk despite his power to control alcohol.

What's at work is the human power to rationalize, to deny realities that we fear would be too painful. Until such a time when it becomes less painful to face them than to pay the huge cost of denial.

a necessary change

John focuses on his own behavior. He's still trying to use his familiar tactics – denial, anger, argument, control - to try to get Jane to be reasonable in terms of sharing parenting,

STILL A DAD

not interfering with his access to his child, and making more reasonable economic demands. And it dawns on him: he has been missing the point that these tactics don't work now and never will, that they are ruining his life.

In this sense, he is like the alcoholic who's deeply unhappy, despairing even, addicted to a false situation, and carrying the sins of the world on his shoulders. The habit of trying to make his life work out by denial, anger, argument and control is very much like addiction to alcohol.

For John, this difficult divorce has been the first time he's had to confront an obstacle frustrating enough that he finally has to come to grips with the fact that these tactics don't work. Before that, he could get away with them... In a way, he's been bullying his way through the current of life, instead of softly navigating the flow, going with the energy. The difficulties of divorce finally opens his eyes. He sees that these tactics that seemed to work so well actually don't work, once the obstacles are bigger. They might actually have been a contributor to his downfall.

He now has to learn new ways – to open his eyes and ears, observe the situation, see what works and what doesn't. It's not going to be easy for John to let go of his wish to control the situation - an understandable desire given the turmoil.

It's going to take a new focus on what makes his life worth living.

a sense of hope

There once was an actor who couldn't use this voice the way he wanted to. He started paying close attention to how he made sounds - not just his voice per se, but also the movements of his body. He kept observing his every movement. And eventually he discovered that he now had an even better command of his body and voice than ever before. So he didn't just go back to the stage; he started teaching his method of movement to the public – it is still taught, to this day, as the Alexander method.

Alexander's story shows the difference between acknowledging our powerlessness and falling into a spiral of despair. When we hit a really difficult spot, many of us start feeling totally overwhelmed. We convince ourselves there's nothing we can do about it or about anything else... We start believing we are doomed. This is not necessarily true.

Alexander's first step was to take stock of reality - the way things were, he simply couldn't be an actor any more. He was powerless in that sense. But he didn't jump to the hasty conclusion that all was lost. He stayed in the simple reality of observing what was happening. He kept trying to move, consciously, focusing his attention on the mechanics and feelings of making movements. He used his energy to deal with the specific problems at hand instead of using it to generate predictions of hopelessness and doom.

Alexander's story is hardly unique. Way back from Antiquity, there are examples of people who have overcome major obstacles through conscious attention. For instance, Demosthenes, born a stutterer, became one of Greece's most famous orators.

At this point, there's not much to lose in trying something new, since the tried and true doesn't seem to be working, anyway. Seeing our powerlessness is not like being stamped as a loser. It's just seeing that our old habits are in the way. As we become more aware that what's going on in our life isn't working, we let ourselves want more out of life. *I've got to try something else, because I deserve a better life. I'm worth it.* We start to have something to look forward to.

It's not that we enjoy the adversity. We're just bowing to the inevitable, and finding how to use it to further our own aims. Since we keep having trouble getting what we want, we'll do our best to use this frustration as a way to grow.

We let ourselves hope.

empowerment

John's capacity to hope is still fragile. Often, something comes about that sends him back into a spin of hopelessness, helplessness, despair.

It all seems to come back down to one scene. It never actually took place as such – but it is very much the way John has been experiencing this divorce process:

The judge says: State your case.
John says: I may be divorcing, but I'm still a parent.
And the judge says: I know parents, and you're no parent.

the knock-out line

Back in 1988, George Bush had selected Dan Quayle as his running mate. The Democratic vice-presidential candidate was a seasoned veteran of politics – Lloyd Bentsen. The public's perception of Dan Quayle was that he was a lightweight – young and inexperienced. He chose to tackle the issue by saying that Jack Kennedy was young, too, when he ran for office. Bentsen's retort came like a slap in the face: *I knew Jack Kennedy. You're no Jack Kennedy.*

Dan Quayle was totally humiliated, reduced to silence. It was a knock-out punch. Bentsen was downright rude and insulting – the sheer audacity of it is what worked. He looked into his opponent's eyes and, in effect, his statement was: *I'm one-up, you're one-down. That's it, and what more is there to say? Your silence confirms the truth of my statement. It's not about being nice – I didn't say anything about being nice. I just stated the truth – I'm up, and you're down.*

This situation creates two roles perfectly made up for each other – like two pieces of a puzzle that interlock perfectly. In the "down" role, all that's left for you is managing the shame and powerless rage. How could you get back at this arrogant son-of-a-bitch, when everything you could say would actually turn back against you – confirming his view of you as an immature, sore loser. People's perception would be that Bentsen got you pegged right – he just put you back where you belong.

Danny boy looking down, trying to be accepted. Patriarch Lloyd Bentsen didn't address the facts, he just played a power play, targeting the weak point: the little child in you who was trying to be accepted. He provided the perfect match for that piece of the puzzle – the perfect complement to the kid who wants to be accepted: the rejecting adult.

Dan: Accept me as a grown-up!
Bentsen: How does one ask?
Dan: Please…
Bentsen: That's not enough.
Dan: Pretty please, with sugar on top.
Bentsen: What kind of a grown-up do you think you are?

how could things be different?

Let's go back to the Bentsen's devastating repartee. What would Jack Kennedy have said if he had been confronted with a barb like the one Bentsen cast at Quayle?

He may not have had to say anything. Maybe just a glance would have been enough: in the fight to be the dominant male, the young, well-endowed male sneers at the old one who is already on his way out. A sneer that would let everybody know how the old man's barb was just an unsuccessful attempt at hiding his fear of the younger man. And the tables would now be turned, with the Bentsen character sulking. How unfair it all was – he had worked a lifetime to get there, and this younger man was getting it all – the charmed life and even the job he had worked so hard, so long to get!

Had Dan Quayle been more confident about himself, things would have been different. He was young, good-looking and rich. Don't you think that, if it were at all possible, Bentsen would have gladly exchanged all his experience and seniority at the senate to be young again, to have Quayle's charmed life?

But Quayle himself didn't value enough what he had, he was more preoccupied with what he didn't have, and so he was vulnerable. He wanted to be what he was not – he thought he had to be what he was not. He felt he needed Bentsen to validate him, to approve of him. It was then easy for Bentsen to have the upper hand – and he found a stinging way to withhold his approval.

As divorced fathers, we may be focusing too much on what we don't have, what we want others to give us, instead of what we have, what they can't take away from us.

john's dream

John had been saying:

Chances are I won't get what I want in terms of involvement with my child and financial arrangement. I can't bear it.

You can't bear it? Are you saying you're going to disintegrate if you don't get what you want?

Well, not disintegrate, but it's gonna be impossible - so hard to deal with...

Can you, for a moment, imagine that you're not getting what you want, but you're happy anyway?

Who do you think I am? Haven't you heard me? Don't you understand how these things are important to me? How could I be happy if I didn't get to see my child? And the humiliation, man, the humiliation! Even thinking of being happy despite that feels like a betrayal. It would be like saying that these things weren't really that important to me! Besides, if I do that, she wins!

Then, John has a dream about losing an arm. A weird thought now occurs to him: *If I had to choose between losing Joey and losing my right arm, I'd rather keep my arm.*

He feels somewhat ashamed of this thought – If Jane knew it, she'd be gloating, feeling vindicated ("Boy, you don't really care that much for your son, do you?").

Nevertheless, this thought has a calming effect on him. Comparing his situation with losing his right arm is not about finding reasons to become less involved in parenting. It's about getting some perspective.

Until then, John's perception of the situation has been: *They're taking everything from me.* They – Jane, the courts. Taking everything from him - not just his child, or his money, but even the sense that he has any right to them. The change this dream is reflecting is greater sense of safety, of wholeness. He's realizing that, even if he loses his child, his money, whatever... he'll still have himself. He'll still have something precious that he doesn't want to lose, something he'll be grateful he didn't lose.

His perspective is changing. What he used to say was: *I've lost everything; whatever I have can so easily be taken away from me.* That is, he was utterly passive, without any power or control. Now, he says: *Maybe, if it had come to a choice between losing my child and losing my arm, I'd have chosen to keep the arm.* Which means: *I still have things I value, I'm grateful for, in my life.*

He's starting to understand that having control is not the

only way he can have happiness. He can find some happiness even if things don't turn out the way he wants. He's letting go of wanting to fully control what he can't control.

It's difficult to be hopeful when we confuse *hoping* with *demanding* that things work out exactly the way we want them to.

settle or fight?

The principle is simple enough – there's a time to fight, and a time to let go. But how will John know when it is appropriate to do one, or the other?

letting go

There is a time and place for letting go of lost causes.

This is not the same thing as hiding a lack of courage behind the pompous construction that "reality" defeats you. This is not the same thing as "managing" a conflict by denying its existence.

Letting go happens after you squarely face the fact that there are areas you don't like (or even hurt you very badly) that you cannot do anything about.

When that happens, you don't avoid the issue: *If I can't have it, I'm not going to dwell very much on whether I want it or not.* Instead, you're conscious of the pain: *I want it very much, and I can't have it.*

Randall writes:

I am a 36 year old divorced father of 2 girls and a boy. I have been divorced for about 3 years. My ex-wife remarried shortly after our divorce, and now has another child by her husband. My ex-wife is very good at manipulating me to the point of upsetting me, she knows what to say, and she does it, in regards to my children, because she knows that's the only way she can get to me. I get very sick of it, these tactics are used quite often when she wants her way. She will try to adjust my visitation, which is set up by the courts as liberal visitation, which we both agreed on, but it seems she doesn't have to always abide with that, if she doesn't get her way, of I don't agree, and go along with her requests. I am sending my children to a private school, she told me last week she was refusing to provide their transportation to and from school, next year, and that she didn't want anything more to do with the school. Her reasoning I was told, she didn't like one of the teachers. I found out my ex-wife was picking up the kids early, peeking in the windows, and disturbing the class before the teachers had finished their closing tasks with my children, and this being very disruptive to the teachers class. The teacher, in a polite, but firm way told my ex-wife that she did not appreciate this type of disruption. This made my ex-wife furious, then she took it out on me, and said she did not want anything more to do with the private school. She wants to always be in control, of every situation. I don't know what to do, I have talked to lawyers, nobody is ever on my side, I am a good father, I love my children more than anything in this world. I take them to church, I am providing a good Christian education for them, I am paying child support faithfully and on time, I have never missed a payment. I do everything the courts and morals require and more that I can do, but it's never good enough for my ex-wife, I am tired of being battered around by her, through my children. If I want to send them to this private school, and I am paying all the expenses, how can she refuse to provide them transportation, for no more of an excuse than being mad at a teacher, in the right, or maybe some school policy that she disagrees with. Please give me some advice as to how to deal with my ex-wife, and this situation, and any legal rights that I may have in this and any verbal abuse and manipulation that she bestows upon me.

It looks like Randall talked to lawyers, and they probably told him the situation is not one that's easy to solve satisfactorily through the courts.

The key to this situation is to for him to keep his focus on something he wrote about her - that *she wants to control the situation.* This is probably very true. Now, she wants it AND she has the means to do so - given the way our divorce system is.

So what can he do?

Remember that, unfortunately, on that point as well as many others, she is in charge and can do pretty much what she wants - regardless of how frustrated that makes him, or how bad it is for the children. Sad to say... but the best way to deal with it is probably with some grin-and-bear-it form of: *Yes, dear.*

Why? If she wants to be in control, and he can't prevent her on these occasions, the best is to relax, because it hurts less.

doubts

Scott writes:

My wife filed for a divorce on my birthday in May 97. I asked why she was divorcing me and her answer was, "Because I don't love you anymore." In the previous year I received numerous cards from her at my business address stating her undying love for me. Now, all of a sudden...

My initial reaction was to fight. My attorney fueled this and believes I have a 50/50 chance of winning custody. I trust her (my attorney) and like her, but am not sure this is the best way to go. Even if I did win, the entire ordeal will take 8 months and $30,000. I determined to settle if my ex would provide a suitable and equitable agreement. She had told me I would receive it on Monday and I agreed to sign it.

While driving, I began trying to visualize non-custodial fatherhood. I won't live with my kids, so that will eliminate incidental contact. All communication will lack spontaneity. It occurred to me, "How can I consider myself their "father" when I don't live with them, mostly communicate by phone and can only see them with permission?" I panicked and depression came over me like a wave.

Today I am with the children and am still indecisive as to whether to settle or fight.

Scott is in a really tough situation. Who wouldn't hesitate? On the whole, though, it looks like his best bet is probably to avoid a long Court battle and to settle.

What he ends up deciding to do is to ask, at the time of the settlement, that his wife and he work out some form of mediation or counseling to define their respective roles. He asks for some counseling now, and for the provision that there can be more later on, as problems emerge.

This costs much less than the Court fight. And, by avoiding the acrimonious fight, he's in a better position to come to agreements that work for both.

wisdom

Wisdom does not lie in meekly accepting every blow. It is not about turning helplessness into a virtue, or calling passivity as a form of moral superiority.

Wisdom is about fighting the battles that need to be fought, as much as it is in knowing which battles are not to be fought.

Conversely, courage is not to be mistaken for indiscriminate bluster. Some men stay locked into desperate legal battles way past the point where they have any hope of anything positive ever coming out of it. Fights fueled only by habit. Fights fueled by the desire to inflict pain - if not on the adversary, then, on oneself. Where there seems to be some kind of perverse enjoyment in "proving" how everything can still get worse - and inevitably will.

How, then, does one know the difference between when

to accept things as they are, and when to push for change?

Wisdom is not something that is magically, suddenly imparted to us. It is a process. We acquire it by making decisions. Some of them work out well; some don't; and that's how we learn. It takes trial and error for us to figure out when courage is called for, and when serenity is of the order. It takes wisdom, from the very beginning, for us to know that we'll be making mistakes along the way. It takes serenity to accept these mistakes, and courage to take their consequences.

This is a process that goes on as long as we are alive. We make the most of it when we grant ourselves the permission to make the mistakes by which we may learn.

It is a conscious process. It requires conscious will and intention. It's not: *Oh, it just happens.* Or: *That's the way it is (and I have no choice…).*

We are aware, active, and we take full responsibility for what we do. We're not trying to force control where it can't work. We're testing reality to see what it is in our power to get, and what isn't.

a moral compass

When John has a low moment – and he's had plenty of them, even moments when he's had fantasies of just going away, far, far away, and forgetting the whole thing – he tries to imagine Joey, grown up, reminiscing about his childhood. He sees Joey saying: *My dad never gave up. I was that important to him.* Then John feels very moved, and very resolute at the same time.

staying the course

There's a moment, in the Odyssey, where Ulysses' ship approaches the island of the Sirens. He knows of the dangers. The Sirens' songs are so beautiful, so seductive, that even the most hardened of sailors lose all control; they steer toward the island and die a horrible death as they are hurled by gigantic waves onto the rocks.

Ulysses knows he'll be powerless over the Sirens' songs, but he also wants to hear them. So he devises this clever trick. He has his sailor fill their ears with wax, so they are totally deaf. He has himself tied solidly to the ship's mast - with instructions to his men that no one untie him until after the ship is well past the island, no matter how much he may beg them or threaten them.

We're human, we'll be tempted to go the easy way, the seductive way. It takes wisdom to know our limitations and to know we'll have to find ways to deal with them.

When they realize how much power their wives have within the system, many fathers are cowed – they fear that, if they displease their wife, they might effectively lose access to their children. Some fathers even rationalize that this attitude gives them a moral victory: *I'll give in, I'll let her have it all, and I'll have the moral high ground.* The trouble is, the mother believes all along that *she* has the moral high ground. So this attitude works just as badly as that of people who commit suicide to show *them* how bad *they* are (whoever *they* are)… it's tragically useless. One does not gain the moral high ground just by virtue of being trampled.

While it is wise to respect the reality of the mother's power, it certainly doesn't mean just becoming a doormat. It may be difficult for a while, but the following comment

from Luke C. illustrates the payoff of not letting himself be
intimidated:

*My ex-wife's attorneys advised her to claim sole legal custody
even though she knew that my son would benefit from having
me remain involved as a full parent. After it was over, she apol-
ogized for this, as well as for making allegations of spousal abuse
which were false. Although we argued over my access to my son
during the divorce proceedings, my ex-wife now expresses great
satisfaction with our joint-custody arrangements and my son's
favorable adjustment to living with two households.*

they can never take that from you

They may take your money, and they may even take your
child. But there's one thing they can never take away from
you. You'll always be your child's father – from close or from
afar. It may not be easy, it may not be the way you had wanted it to be, but his father you are, and forever you will be.

This is an unshakable certainty that helps you confront
challenges. What you're now fighting for is not the right to
be a parent – you *are* a parent, no one can take this away
from you. What you're fighting for is for better conditions in
which to be a parent. In a way, it could be said you are fighting for comfort, for better conditions, as opposed to fighting
for survival. So you can feel less threatened.

Your basic right, to be a parent, is not your wife's – or the
courts - to grant or deny. It exists, naturally, because you're
the child's father. The strength of this right comes from the
depth of your commitment to it.

a conscious relationship

Divorced dads may be even more committed to their children than parents whose right to parent hasn't been challenged. Of course, we can no longer take the relationship for granted. We cannot take for granted that we'll have unlimited amounts of time – that there will always be time for saying or doing the important things.

Now, we have to figure out what's really important: what means a lot to us; what we want to have give our children; what gives us pleasure during the relationship...

We may not have chosen to do it that way (and, if we had a choice, we might still prefer to have it the easy way)... but we might as well see the good side of the situation we're in, see it as an opportunity to have a more conscious relationship with our children.

We are more conscious of the value of this bond – for we have reaffirmed the strength of our commitment in a conscious way, and geared our lives to that end – the same way as somebody who's been close to death values life even more for knowing how precious it is. We're like born-again fathers.

real relationships

There are parents whose children are born handicapped. Many of them, understandably, feel singled out by fate and fall into despair. Others accept that their child is different from what they would have wished a child to be. They take the time to figure out what to do for him and get good at it.

Instead of spending the rest of their lives lamenting how

their situation as a parent is not an enviable one, they face the reality of their own parent-child relationship. Their reality is not being the parent of an ideal child, or even of an average child. It is being the parent of a handicapped child.

John's reality is to be a father in a situation that has a built-in handicap. And his challenge is to make the most of it.

Regardless of how little time he actually gets to spend with his child, he's still a father. He may not be the father he wanted to be, it may not be the relationship he wanted to have... but this is as real a father-child relationship as any. John may call it frustrating, maddening, saddening... it may be all that, but it certainly is not unreal. It is *his* reality.

It's easy to spend a lot of time dealing, not with the reality of your situation, but with your ideas of how it should be. Life becomes simpler when you accept that what is as a starting point for your actions, as opposed to what should be.

**part four:
divorced-fathering**

The clock keeps ticking. Joey keeps growing up. Soon, he's a teen-ager, then he's gone. When these thoughts cross John's mind, he gets scared. He is missing out on his son's childhood, on the opportunities to teach him, to have significant moments with him, to have fun with him… time is slipping by and that never come back…

And yet, as John Lennon said, *Life is what happens when you're busy making other plans.* Life is happening indeed – even if it's not the way John wanted it to be.

being a father

We believe people expect us to live up to the image of the all-powerful, all-giving father. We try to do that, and we disappoint them, as well as ourselves (as we inevitably must).

Unfortunately, to the extent we believe we should be able to live up to this image, we "volunteer" to eventually play the role of bad guy, of deadbeat. This is the reverse image, the shadow, of the powerful and giving father. As a result, we end up being defined by our shortcomings.

Our task, then, is to reconnect with the depths of who we are. We affirm our right to be fathers by exercising it – in the best way we can at the time. We may be fathers with a handicap… we remain fathers. We give all the love we can.

We define ourselves by what we can give, not by what we can't.

advice

In this section of the book, we will be observing John as

he struggles with how to live here and now. We will be seeing how following the inner path he started on earlier influences how he acts as a father. Does this mean this section is
a guide on being a divorced father? On the one hand, it is -
I believe it gives sound advice. On the other hand, to the
extent that it is advice, it is at odds with the approach I am
advocating in this book.

This approach essentially consists in seeking inside ourselves for the inner truth that gives us strength and purpose.
The problem with advice is that it given from the outside.
Blindly following somebody else's rules, however good they
may be, is not conducive to finding our inner truth.

Advice means telling you what to do. The fact is, I don't
really know what *you* should be doing. I am telling you about
my belief system. Hopefully, as you read what I write, you
compare what *you* would do in a similar situation to what
I'm describing. In other words, I hope this book helps you
become more conscious of what you do, more aware that
you may have other options...

focus on the child

John is caught in a system that constantly reminds him of the power and control struggle he has with his ex, so he tends to be obsessed with her. It's hard not to be reminded of the frustrations of dealing with Jane, how she makes life difficult for him, and how much he has lost in the relationship with his child.

John's relationship with his child feels artificial compared to what it used to be when he was functioning as a full-fledged parent. He has lost a lot of his authority – Joey knows that most of the rules governing his life are his mother's doing, not his father's. Joey can also see how his mother openly taunts his father – how she often does the opposite of what he'd want her to do. John has become less relevant to his child's everyday reality – at times, he feels more like an uncle than a father.

As a result, even with the best intentions, his child's presence tends to remind John of these frustrations. And he loses focus on his child.

focusing

It's difficult for John loosen the grip that Jane has on his mind, difficult to let go of thinking about that powerhouse... He knows, somehow, that it's not right – that, when he is with his child, he should really *be* with his child, not with his problems.

He *should* be with his child... but how can he do this? One thing is clear: as long as he deals with this as a *should*, it's yet another obligation for him.

So, first, John has to let go of the *should*. Which means: he relaxes the pressure he puts on himself to do the right thing, he allows himself to first observe what happens.

He is with his child, and he *notices* that his mind wanders to thoughts and frustrations. He *notices* that he is not fully present, yet he does not berate himself for this.

It is true that it is important for him to be fully present, mentally and emotionally, when he is with his child. But: how can present can he really be for his child if he is not present for himself? How truly loving can he be to his child, if he is not compassionate and loving to himself? Keeping a focus on his child doesn't mean losing himself.

Then and only then - when it comes from inside of him - can he be truly there for his child.

expressing feelings

John is trying so hard to be the father he thinks he should be… that his child doesn't always get to see who he really is. Slowly, he has come to understand that, in order for Joey to know him, he has to let him see more of his feelings and emotions.

This was much harder in the midst of the harshest battles of the divorce. John used to fear (maybe with good reason) that, if he let go of his guard, his raw feelings would come out, and they would be terrifying and destructive to his child.

As John is getting more of a handle on his emotions, he is becoming less afraid of revealing more of them to his child. He is more aware of a middle ground. For instance, when Joey says something that hurts him, he can tell him that he feels hurt – silence is not the only alternative to uncontrollable pain or destructive anger.

As John keeps revealing more of himself, he feels emotionally closer to his child. He finds it easier to show his love for him – hugging him, telling him he loves him, but also in many other ways. He has to expend less energy on keeping a lid on his feelings, so he has more to invest in being attentive to his child. He has more warmth to encourage him to do what he likes to do.

asking questions

John has always been interested in Joey's life. He is even more curiosity about it now that he sees Joey less often. Unfortunately, what seems to be happening is that, the more John asks questions, the more Joey clams up.

What seems to work best is when John asks open-ended questions: it's an opportunity for Joey to express himself freely.

Feeling welcomed and loved, sensing his dad's willingness to listen to him, do much more to get Joey to open up and talk to him.

Maybe that is when he feels that dad is really open to him, not questioning him to determine whether or not he approves of him.

The same goes for lecturing - children often say of their fathers that *he talks too much, he doesn't really listen.* It may be that men tend to express their love by giving advice. If so, there are other ways we can show our love.

By the way, "don't lecture" doesn't mean "don't explain" – just don't talk too much. "Don't lecture" doesn't mean "don't discipline" either - just try and do it with fewer words.

other involvements

As John's child grows up, so grows the boy's involvement with other activities. John knows it would happen whether or not the parents were divorced. But he cannot help seeing this as a further encroachment on his already limited time with Joey.

This puts him in an untenable position. In a way, he'd want to lean on Joey to get him to curtail his outside activities. He feels the connection he has with his son is at least as important as many of these activities.

But he also feels happy and proud to see his child growing up and involved with his peers. In fact, when he starts to think about this from Joey's point of view, his own sense of loss subsides.

What happens is: he understands his child's need instead of feeling deprived because of it.

honesty

There are plenty of times when John doesn't know how to handle a given situation. Now that's not something that's unique to divorced fathers – all parents go through that. What makes it harder on John is that he sometimes feels compelled to be the "father knows best" that he cannot be.

To avoid falling into this trap. John gains time by saying: *I don't know how to handle this situation.* He then thinks out loud some options, showing his child what he is considering, revealing his process.

In doing this, John is making himself more visible, hence more vulnerable. He is forsaking the sense of safety that comes from being hidden. This loss has a major compensation: he is emotionally closer to his child.

With older children, it helps to admit that you don't have that much control over your child (just as we don't have that much control over many things in life and divorce in particular).

Instead of rigid rules that can't be enforced, try an honest dialogue. This approach goes for any parent of a teen-ager. It applies even more to non-custodial parents who cannot rely on intimidation and old habits to enforce rules. Children know that their divorced dads don't have that much say over their day-to-day lives. It's frustrating – it would be much easier for you to be able to say: *do it, or else*. But, eventually, all parents have to confront that. You just come to this situation earlier, and more often.

In this sense, being a divorced father prepares you better to being the parent of a grown-up – relinquishing control over him, treating him with respect, and influencing him through moral authority, love and mutual respect more than through old fashioned authority (*you'll do it my way, or else*).

discipline

Divorced fathers are sometimes derisively referred to as "Disneyland Dads" – they just want to have fun with their children, and don't do the hard work of disciplining them. Of course, this is not a fair criticism: being a non-custodial father makes it hard to exercise authority and to discipline your child. Plus, when you don't see your children much, it's understandable you'd put emphasis on having a good time together rather than dealing with unpleasant stuff. But children need discipline from their father, they need to know what he sees as right and wrong (without being lectured!).

What is discipline? Often, the word has a very negative connotation – essentially, that of punishment. But punishment is only one among many possible ways to create discipline. Essentially, discipline means setting limits, defining the bounds of what is appropriate and what is not. This, in and of itself, is not harmful – harm comes from setting boundaries that are too tight, too rigid. Appropriate boundaries give children a sense of security.

When it comes to enforcing discipline, you have less flexibility, fewer tools than your ex. You may feel you have none. But you actually do.

For instance, one way to foster discipline is to model for your children the appropriate behaviors you want to follow. In a way, this is what this journey is all about – finding in yourself the moral compass that guides you, and living your life in harmony with this inner sense of truth and goodness.

staying in touch

Many divorced fathers find it very painful to talk about parenting – it reminds them of how little time they get to spend with their children, how little opportunity they have to actually parent them.

How do you strengthen your relationship with your child when you see so little of him? In many ways, the same rules apply as in any parenting situation. The big difference is – you have fewer opportunities to get involved with your child, so you have to make the most of them.

Many fathers find ways to be creative in going around obstacles. They express their love in many unspoken ways – in making sure to give their children the food they like, in what they read to them... Bob H., a father whose children live too far for him to see them regularly, has been recording himself reading stories, and sending them the cassettes.

Izzy writes:

I call twice a week, I'd call more often, but the phone bill gets too high. I call every Tuesday evening, and one day on the weekend (phone rates are cheaper). I try to mail something once a month. I know this sounds corny, but I bake and mail them cookies, or blueberry bread. The kids get a big kick out of it.

overcoming obstacles

Jim H. says: *I can call you in the evening to see how your day went.* And his daughter replies: *Mom doesn't let me answer the phone when she knows it's you.*

After a while, father and daughter develop a routine. Jessica now knows that, when the phone rings, unanswered, around 6 in the evening, it's her father saying hello to her with the ring itself, if not in words.

This poignant example brings up a lot of questions. Why can't the mother be more cooperative? Shouldn't she let the child talk to her father?

True, but what can you do about it? What is making a change for Jim and his daughter is that Jim is focused on his goal – to stay in contact with his child. He puts his energy into reaching this goal.

staying close

There's no formula guaranteeing a healthy parent-child relationship, even when you're the custodial parent, even when you're still married. You do what you can to be available for what opens up for you and your child.

What counts is that, in the long run, your child feels: *Dad loves me.*

loyalty conflicts

One frustration too many, and the whole line of dominoes of all frustrations past and present falls – John is right back in the midst of the quagmire, he loses all his hard-won wisdom. He thinks Jane richly deserves to be exposed for who she is: *It's high time Joey knew the truth! High time he saw her for who she really is!* Certainly not the all-loving, selfless mother she claims to be. But the last thing Joey needs is for the battle to escalate: *You thought I was the bad guy? Here's what a real bad guy is. Just listen to the latest about your mother!* Children of divorce are torn between two parents fighting for their allegiance. It's an untenable position. So John bides his time. He remains silent, when he wants so much to say:

Look at what your mother did....

For all the pressures he's under, he knows Joey's under even more pressure.

avoid loyalty conflicts

You know better than to put your children in the middle. And yet, there come situations where this seems to happen. For instance, when the mother interferes with your time with your child. It's so tempting then to complain to him: *Your mother is bad for not letting us spend time together.*

Children don't want to abandon one parent in order to be with the other. Instead of hearing how the mother is bad for not letting the two of you spend time together, they'd rather hear that you love them and see that you enjoy spending time together. So... make an effort to shift your focus away from your anger toward the mother, and focus on your child: *I was here last Saturday. Sorry you couldn't come. But I'm happy you're here now.*

Let your focus be on the child, as opposed to against the mother. Be there for your child, until such a time as, being older and able to fend for himself in the world, he no longer needs to defend against the knowledge that his mother is not all-loving and not always right.

don't ask the child to protect you

Children are acutely sensitive and understand more than we often give them credit for. As they watch you and listen to what you say, they can pick up your feelings. If your message to your child is: *I can't see you because your Mom won't let me*, or *The court won't let me*, he'll hear your powerlessness, your desire to be understood and pitied by him. Now, he's not your father, he's your child. You're here to protect him, not the other way around. He may act sympathetic, but you're leaving him with a big void where there's a need for him to feel the reassuring presence of a protective father.

What if your child is upset about what his mother is doing, if he sees the unfairness of her behavior and resents missing the visit? Given all you've been through, it's tempting to see this as an opening to finally rush in with explanations that will "enlighten" your child. For instance: *She's doing that to get back at me through you.* That's probably true… but the point is, it's better to focus on your child's feelings, to let him know you see he's upset, to show him you understand, and, most of all, that you're happy to be with him now.

Your child lives primarily with his mother and is dependent on her for taking care of him, for ensuring the stability of his life. If you destroy her in his eyes, what does he have left?

Now, you may say: *It's her fault, she's the one preventing me from being there for him. My child should know the truth.* Or: *It's the system's fault, depriving kids of their fathers.* And you'd be right – the mother and the courts are certainly making it very difficult for you to be a father. But what would you rather achieve… that your son pity you for being victimized?

Or that he grow up a more secure person, for feeling your ability to be there for him in at least some way, despite the circumstances?

Asking your child to, in effect, protect his father by taking your side against his mother is not going to give him much of a sense of confidence in the world. If a grown up, his father, needs the protection of a child, what is there in this world to grow up for?

Besides, asking him to be the judge of how badly his mother behaves is asking him to play an adult role - in effect to be more adult that you and his mother have been.

let your children be children

All too often, children of divorce seem to act more mature than their age (this can happen in conjunction with acting, at times, in very immature ways).

Psychologists have coined a word for what happens to children who grow up too fast: parentification. When parents are dying, or are fighting so much that they're essentially out of the picture, the kids are essentially on their own. Children of divorce grow up fast because they have to, because there's a vacuum to fill – their parents are children.

This false maturity is a curse rather than a blessing: the children are being robbed of their childhood. Children deserve to be child-like, if not downright childish. If they're too reasonable, it's probably in direct proportion to how childishly their parents are behaving, creating a vacuum they have to fill.

Children are highly resilient to trauma – there's a lot they can handle and overcome. But is this what you'd like their childhood to be?

So, when you catch yourself trying to elicit sympathy for your plight from your child, take a moment to question your own motives. Why is it that you want to enlist your child's help in this battle?

why?

It's not just your child who's struggling with loyalty and closeness and betrayal… You are as well. It is totally normal, in your situation, to feel a lot of sadness and anger and jealousy and envy - feelings that belong to a very childlike place in you, a wounded part.. There's despair, too, when you start thinking that you may have, for all intents and purposes, lost your child, irreversibly.

Hector knows it's not really in his child's interest to hear how bad his mother is, so why does he keep doing it? *Because I already lost him. So at least he sees me with some sympathy.*

You have to keep the faith that all's not lost.

feeling replaced

There's a lot of pain, too, when you feel somebody else has been taking your place in your child's life. J. M. writes:

Boy, do I feel strange. Just got back from my oldest daughter's (11) school where she was acting in a play. My ex-wife was there with her fiance and my little daughter (8). As I came in and sat behind them, my little daughter was on this guy's lap and they were whispering something. That really bothered me since I'm very close to my daughters, although I don't have physical custody. I had to signal my little daughter to come over to me and say hi, even though she had already seen me. This guy has the nerve and lack of common or moral sense to display a fatherly attitude towards my daughters with me present. I know I would respect and acknowledge the presence of another dad if I were in the same situation. This guy is a very lucky man tonight because I'm a reasonable and educated man. But I have to tell you, for a split second there I wanted to send this guy to Mars.

The jealousy is all-too understandable, and so is the angry reaction. It's very tempting to want to remove the intruder. But the solution is not to try to keep your children away from their new stepfather. What's happening is that this man is filling a void in the children's lives. Of course, it's unfair and horrible that this void was ever allowed to exist. But, given the circumstances, the best thing to do *for the children* is for you to focus on ways to get closer to them.

fishing for compliments

When you see how happy your child is with you, it's hard not to ask a question that will lead him to say he's happier, or freer, with you than when he is with his mother. In fact, do the opposite. Let your actions demonstrate that you believe in encouraging your child's identification with both parents. Indicate by your receptive attitude that you're willing to hear him say good things about his mother. Talk positively about her – without lying, just focus on those areas where there's something positive for you to say, however reluctantly.

You don't want your child to censor himself with you – nothing good about Mom to be expressed in this house. Even if *she* does that, realize that doing the same thing is not retaliation that hurts her, it hurts your child.

Create a climate where your child can freely open up about the things he likes about his mother – even those things that make you cringe because they indirectly undercut your involvement with your own child. As trust grows, it will eventually be possible for the child to open up more and more to you, including discussing with you the things that trouble him about his mother.

conflict with the child

It's quite obvious that Joey is angry at his father. It doesn't show up in one big outburst, but the signs are there – a recurring surliness, recurring comments… John believes that Joey is seeing the divorce through his mother's eyes – that Joey is angry at him for things that are not his fault.

And yet, in some way, the anger that Joey is expressing is also a mirror of John's own unexpressed anger. At some level, John resents his son – it's all happening because of him; it's because of him that he's at Jane's mercy. These are understandable, human feelings – perfectly acceptable as long as they remain feelings, as long as they are not acted on. But John is uncomfortable about such feelings, because he loves

his son, because he's afraid that feelings such as these might
mean he's less worthy to be a parent. So the feelings remain
unexpressed, even to himself.

Yet, the best thing he can do for himself and his child is
to acknowledge this anger. Acknowledge it - not express it,
not act it out. Acknowledge it to himself, to trusted friends,
to a therapist.

What about acknowledging his anger directly to Joey?
Only to the extent that it comes out of Joey's needs, and certainly not just to relieve the father's need to confess, to
unload his burden. How then?

There are plenty of occasions. What makes it difficult to
see such occasions is that they occur at times when John feels
most vulnerable.

the child's anger

Listen to what's happening.

If your child is showing a lot of anger toward you, don't
be put off by it. It's understandable that you'd be upset about
it. But, when you act upset, you are giving him the message
that his expression of anger is not welcome. You might also
be subtly trying to demonstrate to him that he's wrong to be
angry at you. You'd be dealing with the manifestation, not
the underlying causes. If, instead, you listen to him, you'll
understand what's really happening underneath, and you'll
be better able to eventually find a way to solve the problem.

It's difficult to do so because it's difficult not to feel defensive when your child is angry at you. Plus, it all seems like it
depends on causes that are beyond your control, and basi-

cally brings you back to the frustration of the lack of power you have in this situation, and the misuse of power by the child's mother.

One thing that helps dealing with the anger is to reframe it. Think of anger as a warm emotion, compared to coldness and distance. When your child is angry, the good news is he's showing you his feelings instead of keeping them to himself, having written you off as somebody unimportant, or too rigid to allow it (*what's the point of even showing my anger to Dad?*).

Where there's anger, there's still hope.

the confrontation

Joey often complains that his father yells at him. John feels that he never yells, and certainly not at his son: *I just make such an effort to stay calm and collected with him. Even when there is so much in my life that I could explode about!*

He feels hurt that Joey sees him in such a distorted way. He feels angry at Jane. *This must be her doing, once again. Even if she's not directly responsible for this, she is indirectly - by fostering a situation where Joey has to choose between two parents, must make Mom into the good one, and the Dad into the bad one...*

Now, there may be truth to all this. But what is John actually going to do? He's tempted to argue, to try to prove to Joey that he never yells. What if he had a video camera to record his moments with Joey? At the end of the evening, he'd play it back for him: *See, no yelling!*

This, of course, is absurd. If Joey's perception of his dad

is that he's yelling, all the video would show is that, this one time, or that other, Dad happened not to yell.

Or would it even do that? Wouldn't Joey just perceive the tension in John's voice, the twitches in his mouth, as anger? Seeing a glimpse of his Dad's very real anger (his anger at Jane, at life..), and misinterpreting it as anger directed at him…

What can John do? Even though he feels that, of this one thing at least, he is totally innocent, he nevertheless apologizes to Joey for yelling at him.

And he's very surprised. He expected to feel bad for "admitting" doing something bad. Instead, he feels a warm glow – he feels generous. He's given his son something that really meant a lot to him. He didn't humiliate himself, he gave a gift. Now, he feels much closer to Joey. He's also sorry that Joey felt threatened by what he had done.

And the funny thing is: acknowledging the yelling that had never happened opens a door for him to start dealing with the real tension that exists between him and his son. And to start dispelling it.

if you feel totally powerless

If you truly feel that there is nothing you can do, that your child will not listen to you at all… this is an alarm signal. Not necessarily in the sense you'd think – *what's wrong with the little monster?*

One avenue to explore is: *In what way am I starting to project overwhelming power onto him? In what way am I not seeing him as my child, or even as a human being, but just as a*

*powerful creature that has no love and respect for me, and is out
to get me?*

Chances are, in such a situation, you are not dealing with
some of your own anger, your sense of being victimized in
life and in your divorce in particular, your sense of being
powerless and overwhelmed. Chances are it's difficult for you
to separate your feelings from your child's.

It would do you good - and do your child good – if you
found ways to express more of your anger (probably not with
him, at least at first). Do so in a safe setting, e.g. in therapy,
or within a support group, where you can explore it without
adverse consequences. After all, if you have not been expressing your anger, you have deep fears about how it may pro-
voke dire consequences, and you don't want to be proving to
yourself that these fears are true.

Once you become more comfortable with this anger, you
will find ways to be more assertive with your child – to be
there for him and also be yourself. This, in turn, will change
the relationship.

There's a lot you can learn from that perspective, that can
help you change your part of the dance you're involved in
with your child. While the child's role may be to start the
dance – it's up to you to be aware of how you stay in it.

**part five:
toward peace**

When we first met John, he was prey to all sorts of anguish, a tormented man. He was deeply involved in the adversarial struggle with Jane as well as the struggle between Good & Evil raging inside himself. By now, however, a noticeable change has taken place. There's a clear sense that John has more peace of mind – a physical sense that the pressures have eased off, that he almost literally has more room to maneuver.

Are we there yet? Is the end of the journey in sight?

It would really be nice if there was a way to come to an end - the aspiration to Nirvana: once we've reached it, no effort is necessary any longer. Bliss without pain. Happy ever after.

But the end-result of this process has an intangible, elusive quality. It's not like a medal or a diploma we acquire and then is ours to display forever. We have to keep working at it.

Say we start a program of physical exercise "to get fit". We won't stay fit unless we keep exercising. And there's more chances we'll keep exercising if we actually enjoy the exercising itself, as opposed to feeling it's something we have to do only as a means to an end.

We gain a sense of feeling actively responsible for our own life - as opposed to dwelling mostly on those parts of our life where we have little or no control. We may at times feel very hurt… we allow ourselves to experience pain and anger. But we're not making "victim" our identity.

When we start changing deeply, it's not just in one separate compartment of our lives. It's reflected, in some way or another, in all that we do. This process is about opening up more and more, in contrast to the hunkering down we experienced as we felt attacked from all sides, when we felt we had little rights and even less protection.

We experience difficulties, we catch ourselves reverting to the old habits, the defensive postures… The difference is, we now make the conscious decision to go beyond these defensive reflexes.

conflict with jane

John sees Jane as the scary teacher who is pointing a finger at him, blaming him for not being good enough. He feels his fear of her is all the more justified because Jane's point-of-view has powerful allies in Court.

The scariest part of the story, however, is that Jane is actually as scared of him as he is of her. Jane's fear is not caused by violent acts, or by threats of physical violence (although this can happen in some divorces as well as some marriages). Her fear of John is the mirror image of his fear of her. She sees him as a scary parent type, garbed in self-righteous outrage, blaming her for not being good enough. She hears him blaming her for depriving her son of a father.

So there you have these two scared children in adult bodies. That's John and Jane trying to hide their fears behind the intimidating mask of self-righteous, blaming parents. Blaming each other. Scaring each other.

Blaming somebody else - no matter how richly they deserve it - does not get us closer to getting what we really want out of life. For instance, what happens when John blames Jane or the system? He says: *But, in this case, the blame's justified. If it weren't for her, we'd have a reasonable and sensible divorce. If only this were an even playing field...*

But, John, are you doing that well for yourself with this attitude? Is it succeeding in giving you what you want - in court, in talking to your ex, in the way you experience your life?

Hey, but it works so well for her, it's the way she gets everything.

Yes, but does it work for <u>you</u>? Is it possible that this "victim" stuff is something you think ought to work for you... but doesn't actually work?

Not really. It's more like - I'm up to my neck in this morass of blame and finger-pointing - she's doing it, the courts encouraged it - it has become a way of life. I don't really think about acting differently any more.

John, you don't have to keep living this way. You don't have to buy into the logic of the adversarial divorce system that promotes nasty fighting – the legal construct that there has to be a good parent and a bad one. So why are you so much involved in dishing out blame? I don't mean stop fighting unilaterally in court – you may very well have good reason to protect yourself. I mean, stop to see how much energy you're putting into deflecting blame and dishing out blame.

John, listen to Joey. When you're in your dark clouds - your complaining and unhappy mood – how relaxed are you with him? Are you really there for him – or are you mostly brooding about what you've lost, what feels hurtful or infuriating to you?

John, when you're like this, it's as if you were giving Jane free access to your mind, inviting her inside to torment you. Worse - it doesn't even cost her any effort to do that: it's all happening inside your own mind.

You're telling yourself scary stories that make you feel more and more miserable, in a whiny, relentless, endless sort of way. The misery that comes from these thoughts seems to never die. Thoughts always reactivate it - they actually keep feeding it, just like the wind can activate a fire. And so these thoughts keep nagging you – rubbing your nose in your powerlessness.

Is this the life you want to have?

mirror images

Both sexes often feel powerless over the other. Men feel powerless over women – especially in a divorce. But many women feel helpless about what they see as men's power. They'll complain that other women give more authority to what a man says than to what a woman says.

We all fall into the trap of losing our own authority, projecting it somewhere else, and being scared by its reflection.

What's strange – tragic, even – is that men and women

are not talking about the same thing. They don't see each other. They see their own fears reflected in the other.

The woman sees an overwhelmingly strong man, a potential abuser. She sees him as somebody who doesn't really care about the children, just pretends he wants to be with them to shirk his financial obligations.

The man sees a manipulative witch who uses her alleged weakness as a tool to gain power. He sees her as holding the kids hostage.

We make our worst fears come true. The woman attacks the man, keeps the children, makes it difficult for him to see them, and then complains she has the unenviable task of being a single mother.

The man fears she'll take advantage of him and humiliate him, and she does, taking his kids as well as his money and authority. She emasculates him under the guise of asking him to be a man, not a woman-like nurturer.

how can you get her to...

You ask yourself: *How can I get her to sit down and talk?* She doesn't want to, and nobody's forcing her to. You feel your child is held hostage by her. What was a battle between you and her has turned into a battle where the children are the battlefield. You see her hiding behind the child to get what she wants: her pain is described as the child's pain.

You have no control over her. You can't force her to *be reasonable* (she certainly wouldn't agree that reasonable is the right word for what you want), or even talk.

If only I could get her to agree to mediation... this is the kind of thinking that keeps you firmly entrenched in the game, the dance you're playing with her, where you keep feeling powerless without alleviating her own sense of powerlessness and defensiveness.

a way out of the game

A person who keeps repeating the same thing is somebody who doesn't feel heard. This goes for her (why does she keep saying the same thing over and over again?). But this also goes for you (you too keep repeating the same thing to her).

You feel unseen, unheard. So you neither see nor hear her. To change the dynamics of the situation, start doing something different. Try to see her, to listen to her,

Why wouldn't you? Do you feel one-down when you feel she doesn't listen to you and you have to listen? Well, you *are* one-down. Nothing new there, this is unfortunately the reality, for men, of divorce American-style.

So, go back to what your priorities are. Is it more important for you to deal with the pecking order, or to achieve better parenting conditions? For the latter, you need to establish a dialogue with has a habit to not collaborate and, given the system you're operating under, feels she has nothing to lose by not collaborating.

Having feelings about it is understandable. But you may decide not to act on these feelings if your primary goal is more important – your focus is on remaining as involved in your child's life as you can be.

Another obstacle is that, by now, you have assumptions of

how she's going to treat you. It's hard to start with an open mind, to assume she's going to be receptive to what you say. It may take her time to recognize you're genuinely listening when you are, and she may at first be distrustful and unreceptive (as in: *get lost!*).

It's not going to be easy, there will be plenty of setbacks to discourage you. So you need to keep in mind why you want out of the blaming game: it is a game where you're bound to lose. There is also a deeper reason. The blaming game, the adversarial divorce, are destructive practices. Where there once were two respectable parents, you now have two enemies throwing mud at each other, succeeding in exposing each other's worst side – and, in the process, showing their own childish destructiveness – the very opposite of the parental qualities they'd like to instill in their children. Behaving like unruly nasty kids instead of responsible parents. And that's not what you really want, is it?

train yourself to listen to your ex

You don't know what's in her mind. Stop pretending you do. Train yourself to ask: *Are you saying…* and repeat what she just said. *Are you saying, in the context of our finances, that I could pay more?*

At this moment, you're really trying to hear what she's saying. You're not trying to change her mind to what you believe is the right way. Of course, the tone of voice is important. We're talking about a tone that conveys an honest interest in hearing and understanding her position, not a sarcastic comment on her lack of realism.

Instead of confronting her, ask her: *Are you saying that, because you carried the child, you should have custody?* What does she really want? Maybe not as much custody as recognition, acknowledgment – from you, but also from the child. Security, material and moral, in a troubled and scary period of her life?

It doesn't mean you don't have the same needs. It doesn't mean you're not entitled to them as well. But, when you recognize what her needs are, you may be in a better position than when you're acting out of your fear of her overwhelming power.

The tragedy of divorce in the current system is that both parents are traumatized and scared of each other.

the unseen mother

Throughout the marriage, Jane wanted John to be as involved as he could possibly be in Joey's life. So what suddenly happened that she seems to be pushing him away? Of course, there's her anger at John, her desire to punish him. But, in punishing him this way, she's also punishing herself – while there are a lot of joys in parenting, there are also many burdens. It is much more difficult to raise a child as a single mother than to share the tasks with a partner.

What Jane says is that she doesn't want John involved because he's wronged her and he's wronged the child. He has not been receptive to her needs or the child's needs. In what way? He hasn't perceived what she needed at a time when she felt really vulnerable, so much in need of support. She has been asking for his support for this new life, she's been explaining to him why she needed his support – she is the child's ultimate support, she cannot do it alone, she needs the father's understanding and support. But all John has been seeing is his own discomfort, his own loss! John is so thoughtless, so selfish. Time and again, he's proved himself to be so destructive that it is better to actually have him out of the family altogether.

Jane feels unseen – what she has been doing as a mother is not acknowledged; she is not valued. If John can have an equal role as a parent, it means that all her pain and suffering and thankless work really isn't appreciated.

She feels she has been doing all the hard work of parenting all through Joey's life. But, when Dad showed up, Joey rushed to the door. Dad tossed him up in the air. Giggles of delight. And Mom, at this moment, felt that the child was more John's than it would ever be hers – bonded by joy, not utilitarian stuff, not guilt – the sheer pleasure of being together and having fun together, of being happy to be alive, of enjoying life together, of having fun with each other. There she was, on the sidelines, doing the thankless tasks that make it all possible, and what would she get for it? To be alone and forgotten as soon as he walks home.

All she's done must not have been worth much, if the father gets the same recognition as a parent by just waltzing into the home and tossing the child in the air. OK, he may also have been feeding him the bottle and changing diapers and all that... but who had to endure the nine months of

childbearing and the labor? That gives you rights, doesn't it?
What's behind Jane's demands is her pain.

Jane would love to hear John acknowledge what she's
been doing, what makes her so special, unique, irreplaceable.

*Yes, Jane, it's wonderful of you to have carried our child. Yes,
Jane, I am in awe of that, this is something that is utterly impossible for me to do.*

*I am envious of the bond you have with our child. Not just
now, when I feel you're holding him hostage. It's much older. It's
because of the closeness that existed between you as far back as
when he was a baby, and even before he was born, when he was
in your belly.*

*I do not claim to be just like a mother – when I say that, I
realize you feel I'm minimizing the importance of those things
you did that I couldn't possibly have done.*

One of Jane's worst fears is that John might very well be
capable of walking away, that Joey does not mean that much
to him anyway. The fear is: deep down, the man doesn't really care about the child. He's free (as opposed to the woman,
who bears the child for 9 months, and then stays the primary caregiver). It costs her nine months of her life– nine
months carrying the baby inside her body. It's her own flesh,
something that's been growing inside her body, fed by her
own body. How can you compare that to the father's contribution – the time it took to get an erection? There might also
be some envy of the man's freedom. In any case, she believes
the man will abandon the wife and kids, unless he's tethered
to the house – or forcibly held to his financial obligations in

the case of divorce.

Usually, this makes John very defensive – he feels blamed, he is described as selfish. The temptation is strong to attack back, or at least act defensive: *No, this is not who I am.*

But, if he focuses on listening to Jane, he can see that what she's voicing under the blame is her fear. She has been so afraid that he could so easily walk away from the child, from his parenting obligations, whereas she was tethered to them.

Instead of responding to the blame, John can validate her fear and address it: *You're right. I could walk away so easily. It's just that I don't want to. I want to be a father. It's a conscious choice. And, maybe, in that, it is more of a deliberate decision than if I had carried a child for 9 months in my body and had breast-fed the child. Maybe, because I don't have to, it actually means more coming from me than from you. After all, how could you help not being involved? For me it's a choice, not a biological knee-jerk reflex.*

Just as, in this day and age of birth control, having a child is a choice instead of a biological imperative, an accident one has no control about.

She might then be more ready to hear John's fears:

What happens to me is, when I hear you say that your pain gives you rights, I start being afraid I'm going to lose any chance to be with my kid – our kid. I hear you saying it's either you or me. I minimize what you did, because I don't want to lose the kid. But, if I don't fear that it will be used as an argument against me, I can relax and admit my appreciation for what you've done, and continue to do for him.

Remember, way back when, it feels like centuries ago, when you were pregnant and I was putting my hands on your belly. Remember how I was in awe of you.

What's happened now is that I am no longer the lone wolf. I am tamed – I am attached to this child of mine. I don't want to lose him.

seeing the deadbeat

John makes a confession:

I was once a deadbeat dad. Well, technically.

Technically?

If you're a divorced father, if you had agreed to pay more in child support than you can afford, then you're a deadbeat dad. It's that simple.

For a while, in the struggle to define the terms of the separation, John withheld payment of child support to Jane. She called him a deadbeat dad - a position he finds emotionally and morally abhorrent.

This is a difficult issue to deal with. Can an honorable man and a loving father ever let himself be in a position to be called, even technically, a deadbeat dad? Is a man truly honest who can be said by others to have committed a crime?

"Deadbeat dad" is a powerful expression. It conveys a mixture of sleaze, irresponsibility and weakness that results in hurting innocent victims. It implies betrayal of the most sacred things, a weakness so hurtful to others that it is criminal. It has an emotional power almost comparable to the abhorrence one can have toward a child abuser.

Betrayal: can one bear to imagine the heartbreak of the child who has come to have a taste of what a dad could be, and whose trust and longing has been betrayed by the disappearance of his dad?

Being a "deadbeat dad" is such a horrible thing that John is balking at identifying himself this way – he's toning it down with the word "technically". There's a whiff of childhood there. The teacher asks the child: *So you lied?* The child replies: *In a way...* The child is evasive. Because he senses he's being accused, not just of committing one wrong action (which, kept in perspective, might not have such dire consequences)... but of having failed to perform as a human being would; of having betrayed the trust of the teacher and of the whole human race, of having fallen from grace. You could admit you did something wrong, once. It's harder to agree that you deserve to be thrown out of the community of humans.

Being in the position to be called a deadbeat dad raises a lot of conflicting emotions in John - guilt and anger among them. It's difficult to deal with these. As a result, he tends to go into a "victim" role. A lot of his energy is spent justifying himself, were it only in his own eyes: What he did was not really his doing, he was pushed to it by the actions of others.

doing the impossible

What happened, how is it that you became a deadbeat dad?

Basically, I needed to reduce my child support payments.

You needed to..?

I really needed to, but I must admit I wasn't unhappy about reducing the payments. I also had wanted to.

Oh, my God, it's so hard to say it. It seems so selfish - the very thing I'm accused of, and I just admitted it, didn't I?

John grimaces with pain as he has a vision of angry Jane, her lawyer, the judge… furiously teaming up on him: *You wanted to reduce your payments, huh? You'd love to reduce your taxes, too, wouldn't you? Well, join the club. We all have obligations that we have to assume. Do you believe people pay their taxes out of pleasure? You're responsible for your kids, and you must assume your responsibility.*

In this context, it's virtually impossible for John to admit to simply "wanting" to reduce child support payments.

The only way I am allowed to ask for a reduction is if I "need" it as oppose to "want" it. And it has to be need beyond the shadow of a doubt. A life or death situation. What I want doesn't count and is selfish.

Fathers should support their children, there's no question about that. What's more questionable is to ask fathers to assume all or most of the financial obligation. And even more questionable to set this obligation at such levels that the father has to become a money-making machine.

pleasure in revenge

There may be satisfaction in getting revenge for what others did to you. Especially during divorce, where your ex has such tremendous capacity to hurt you exactly where it hurts most. And to keep doing it, maddeningly. Or when the judge so callously ignores the reality of your situation. Or even your own lawyer...

These people don't see you, they're treating you like you're not a human being capable of being hurt. So if you can hurt them, in turn, at least you'll stop being a punching bag, you'll show them you exist!

So it's OK to feel there are people you'd love to hurt even more than they've hurt you. It's OK to acknowledge that you want to inflict harm on them. Once you acknowledge the intent to be cruel, you are freer to let go of it. You may actually decide to not seek revenge.

On the other hand, when you don't acknowledge the impulse to be cruel, you can go to great lengths to justify your actions - even just to yourself: *What I did, I did in self-defense.* Or: *OK, I'm not a saint. But wouldn't most people have done just what I did, or actually, even worse? Wouldn't they?*

This is not about being a saint or a sinner. This is about facing reality - whether or not some of your actions did harm to other people.

It's very conceivable that you think about some people: *Yes, I did something harmful to them, and I certainly would do it again, and even harm them more if I could possibly do it.* It is actually *better* to acknowledge your desire to hurt others than to keep saying that you didn't really hurt these people "because it was really their fault". When you say that, you cast yourself in the role of powerless victim. You say you have no power over your actions. You pretend you're such a powerless puppet that even the harmful things you may be doing to your ex are her responsibility!

The point of this process is to help you regain power over the things you can have power about. You may have no power over others - your ex, the courts, the legal system... But you can do something about the way you behave. When you acknowledge that there is some pleasure in your harming others, that it is your way of feeling less powerless... you're no longer stuck on the defensive. You now have a choice between continuing on the same path, or taking another.

There may be some satisfaction in revenge; but, at some point, you may decide that it's not really what you want most out of life...

the wish

Once upon a time, there was a greedy man who found a magic lamp - something like Aladdin's lamp. He rubbed it, and a genie appeared, offering to give him whatever he wanted. You can imagine how the greedy guy's grin was growing by the minute… But there was a catch: whatever he'd get, his neighbor would have two of! The man had to think really hard; he was frowning in intense concentration. Then his face lit up – he was happy, he knew what he wanted to ask: "Make me blind in one eye!"

There may be some satisfaction in striking back, in hurting people. But the energy you put into this distracts you from putting your energy into your own happiness and fulfillment.

letting go

Facing the fact that your actions have harmed some people helps you shift from seeing yourself as a passive, powerless victim. You can now look at your own part in the problem.

What prevents you from doing this?

Earlier, you were so caught up with being judged (and judging yourself) that you couldn't pay attention to much else. As a result, you're holding on to some feelings, some resentments, and probably unexpressed hopes as well. This is the time to face these things. You have a choice - stay where you are, or let go of what's holding you in place.

It's about getting out of your own way.

So, John, let's forget about Jane blaming you. Let's forget about your guilt for a moment. Let's forget whether you had a choice or not, whether "they" pushed you to it or not. Let's concentrate now on whether what you did harmed anybody.

It harmed Jane - she felt she needed more money. And Joey - he felt that his dad didn't love him enough, otherwise I'd have paid what his Mom said was needed.

John, how do you feel about causing them harm? Are you sorry?

For Jane? No way! But for Joey... I feel really sorry that he had this experience. I'm angry at Jane for letting him interpret the situation this way...

But the point is: knowing her, I couldn't expect any other reaction from her. I kind-of-knew it was going to result in this – in Joey thinking I didn't care enough for him to pay. And I am sorry about that.

What you just did is that you acknowledged the hurt that you caused your son. You're sorry about that – and saying so has nothing to do with whether you were right or wrong to do what you did.

This is not about right and wrong – this is about letting go of what's holding you back from having a fulfilling life - for yourself, and your child.

peace

There's often a silent reproach in Joey's eyes – a very expressive way of stating: *I've learned a while back that I can't ask you for anything.* John feels really upset about that. He wants so much to argue - *but you see how I'm here for you – for instance this case, or that case...*

This is not the time to argue, however. This is a signal for John to hear how his child feels - what his experience of their common history has been.

Joey's version of history is that his father hasn't been there when he needed him. He didn't pay the money that was needed for him to live, and his Mom and he suffered from that. What Joey understood at the time, what is now imprinted in his mind, is that Mom was struggling to raise him while Dad was making problems for the family instead of helping.

John is upset that his son is seeing him through Jane's eyes. It would mean so much to him that Joey see him in a favorable light, that he understand his side of the story – it was a fight about money, power and control; there was no other way to deal with Jane. But this is not the time to try to change Joey's view of what happened.

At this point, if John were to argue that "the truth of the matter is...", Joey would just see him as argumentative and defensive. This moment is for John to understand his son and let him know that he understands him.

Joey's truth is that he felt abandoned by his father. Everything else is just words to him.

John, it may very well be true that you did the best you could, and that Jane bears a lot of the responsibility for the way things turned out... but this is not what Joey has experienced. What Joey saw is that Dad did something horrible to the family in general and to him in particular. The most important thing you can do at this moment is to acknowledge his son's feelings: *Yes, Joey, you are right to be hurt and upset. I am really sorry.*

As he says that, John is really sorry that Joey has been feeling hurt. Whether or not he did the best thing he could at the time, it had a cost. It hurt his child then, and it continues to hurt him now. This is certainly not what he wanted to achieve. He is genuinely sorry about that.

a sense of harmony

While John still has to contend with Jane and the courts and the system… he is well on his way to having made peace with the enemy inside. He's been confronting his fear of being evil, the fierce internal critic that would amplify any criticisms he'd hear from the outside to the point where it was deafening, unbearable.

Little by little, he's becoming more accepting of his flaws, defects, defenses… to the point where he doesn't have to deny them. His struggle for self-improvement has shifted. It used to be that he was trying to "become good" – which is another way of saying trying to live up to an outside image of what he should be. He used to try to eradicate the "bad" parts of himself, exorcise his demons.

In other words, he was looking at himself as if from outside, judging parts of him, wanting to kill those parts he deemed undesirable. He's now becoming more accepting of those "evil" parts, seeing them as defenses. Because he's more accepting of these defenses, there's less of a need for him to be defensive when he looks at them. And he's more able to notice that defenses have a cost to him – a cost he may no longer want to pay.

The world outside hasn't changed. What has changed is the way he experiences it. From feeling powerless and victimized, he now feels more at peace with the world.

There are still many things he cannot control. For one thing, he still doesn't have as much of a parent role as he'd like to have. But he has less of a tendency to take that as a personal insult. He tends to get less mired by what frustrates him. He's directing more of his energy in directions where he has some ability to get what he wants.

It's a shift in his focus – he's no longer primarily focused on his own pain. His sense of self goes well beyond a sense of being victimized. And he feels more broadly connected with his fellow human beings - divorced fathers, other men, and women as well.

He can see there is pain in the world other than his. Much of it is much greater than his. He can see that Jane is part of the human race, struggling, dealing with her own pain. Not just bent on hurting him.

He is now freer to seek that which brings joy and fulfillment to his life. And this, in turn, makes him a better role model, a better person to be with, and a better father.

the return of the father

John struggled with the pain and anger of losing his role as a parent. He found out he could turn this into the opportunity to become a more conscious parent.

To do this, he had to become a more focused, more centered person. He had to rebuild himself. This, in turn, lead him to leading his own life in a more conscious manner… and to find more fulfillment in his own life.

Of course, this did not fail to change for the better the relationship he had we with his child – making it deeper, more authentic.

And John now knows that his task as a father is to gently guide Joey toward his own journey, so that he too may feel whole.

**about the journey
from the farther shore**

the hero's journey

Joseph Campbell[11] analyzed myths and legends throughout the world, throughout the ages. He saw that the appeal
of such stories is not just their entertainment value. The
hero's adventures are a magnified version of our process as we
go through life, as we learn from our own trials and tribula-
tions.

Going beyond the obvious differences among the many
stories he reviewed, Campbell discovered many striking similarities. He came to see the *journey* as having a common
structure in all cultures – a structure that reflects the way we
humans deal with the process of overcoming trying circumstances and learning from this experience.

This *journey* is not the stuff of past legends – as opposed
to contemporary life. The archetypal dramas go on – the
characters are the same as ever, what changes is just the sets
and the costumes. Campbell's famous quote illustrates this
point: *The latest incarnation of Oedipus, the continued
romance of Beauty and the Beast, stands this afternoon on the
corner of Forty-second Street and Fifth Avenue, waiting for the
traffic light to change.*

Whether or not we acknowledge the deep resonance of
the *journey* myths, we experience the process of the *journey*
when we confront difficult circumstances that challenge us
to adapt and transform. It's an intensely personal adventure
but, in being so personal, it also connects us to the deep
archetypes of the hero's journey.

In this day and age, the path most commonly used for a

journey of personal growth is psychotherapy – we explore ourselves under the guidance of an experienced traveler. The cognitive maps we use are those of psychology, psychoanalysis and their many branches. The scientific language of these disciplines sometimes obscures the poetic quality of this quest. Consistent with the efficient, technology-oriented culture we live in, we use the medical metaphor of *therapy* to describe this process. The word *therapy* - cure – implies that there is some form of sickness that has to be cured in order for us to function better, and that there is a technology that allows us to do so.

In fact, the healing power of psychotherapy stems in large part from its ability to let us *feel* the poetic quality of the journey of exploration.

the divorced father's journey

One way to describe what we're going through is: a nasty and undignified divorce. Another way is to say that we are also experiencing profound transformations as we face deeply disturbing situations and find ways to respond to them. In that, we are like the heroes of legend – they accomplish the labors that Fate or the Gods bestowed on them and, in the process, find themselves.

Like so many of these heroes, we visit the circles of Hell, we enter the heart of Darkness. Facing these travails helps us understand who we really are. We realize what our priorities are - where we draw the proverbial line in the sand, what we're willing to passionately commit to.

Even the turmoil, the craziness and the undignified

moments take on a spiritual dimension. The sacred is not out there, in a sphere far removed from the ordinariness of everyday life. The journey starts when we begin to notice the sacred where it is - among all the misery and shabbiness of the here and now.

And, when we realize this, we have reached our destination.

appendix:

report of the u. s. commission on child and family welfare, september 1996

The Commission on Child and Family Welfare was established by Congress in the Child Support Recovery Act of 1992. The Commission received a broad charge to investigate a wide variety of issues that affect the best interests of children and provide recommendations to the President and the Congress.

The 15 Commissioners were sworn in on January 10, 1995. The 15 Commissioners brought to the table their own expertise and specific concerns - spanning family law, children's issues, mental health, domestic violence, and child and family welfare, with expertise in both research and delivery of services. The Commission heard national experts, parents, and other concerned citizens and representatives of community-based organizations that educate and assist parents and children who are experiencing the effects of divorce and single parenthood.

The following provides extracts from the Commission's reports. The complete texts (majority and minority reports) are available on the internet:

(http://www.erols.com/afc/usccfw.html).

the commission's conclusions

In charting its course, the Commission had to try to reconcile strongly held viewpoints on the family, marriage, parenting, divorce, unmarried parents, father absence, and outcomes for children. These viewpoints often were at odds with one another. Yet, the Commission's members found enough common ground to conclude that:

- "the evidence is clear that most children do best when they receive the emotional and financial support of both parents"

- "the confrontation of parent against parent, especially if it is ultimately resolved in litigation in which there are winners and losers, simply is not a good way to induce cooperation between parents and best address the interests of the children"

The Commission clearly identified the terms of the debate, contrasting the good behavior of divorcing parents who cooperate and create parenting plans vs. the devastating aspects of the adversarial system:

"...Many divorcing parents focus on the interests of their children. They try to assure that their separation has a minimal impact on their children. They work together to provide adequately for their children. They plan together how to share decision-making about the children's schooling, religious upbringing, medical care, and participation in activities. They agree on what rules and kinds of discipline should be used with the children. They agree on where the children will live and they make reasonable arrangements about sharing parenting time.

"...For other parents, divorce is a paralyzing experience... Although in many divorcing families there is hostility before the decision to divorce, the divorce often heightens the hostility. The parents vie for the loyalty of their children. One parent may use control of the children to the exclusion of the other parent as a source of power and security; another parent may use control of financial resources to achieve the same ends. Often, anger toward each other is used as justification for lack of cooperation. Too often, the parent who does not live with the children fades from their lives. It has been well documented that children in such hostile situations pay a price.

"...When separating, divorcing, or unmarried parents cannot reach agreement on parenting issues involving their children, they must often resort to an adversarial system that dies little to ensure that they come to terms with their changing situation and feel comfortable with the outcome.

specific recommendations

"Therefore, the Commission, as its mission, sought ways of creating environments in which decisions can best be make about the well-being of children to ensure they receive the emotional and financial support of both parents.

"In particular, the Commission decided to focus on custody and visitation issues that affect the children of separating, divorcing, and unmarried parents. ...The Commission looked for ways to reduce the adversarial nature of court proceedings affecting parental decision-making, parenting time, and residential arrangements of children whose parents are separating, divorcing, or unmarried. "

Among its recommendations were the following:

- "Courts and legislatures should replace the terms "custody" and "visitation" with terms that more accurately describe parenting responsibilities and are less likely to foster conflict, such as "parental decision-making," "parenting time," and "residential arrangements" for children. (Recommendation 1)"

- "Courts should require separating, divorcing, and unmarried parents living apart to attempt to develop parenting plans that set forth parental decision-making, parenting time, and residential arrangements for the children. Courts should provide guidance for the development of parenting plans by identifying the legal parameters and issues that plans should address and by making forms available to help parents develop the plans. (Recommendation 7)"

- "Courts should require separating, divorcing, or unmarried parents living apart who have not agreed on a parenting plan to try to resolve their differences through mediation, except in cases involving domestic abuse, substance abuse, mental impairments, and/or other characteristics of the parties that would make mediation inadvisable or that would preclude a fair mediation process. (Recommendation 8)"

minority report

The following provides extracts from a Minority Report by John Guidubaldi, D.Ed,, L.P., L.P.C.C., Commissioner, U.S. Commission on Child and Family Welfare.

"Frustrated attempts to resolve our disparate points of view sometimes led to political expediency and watered down recommendations. On several critical issues, rather than offering the President , and Congress clear suggestions for change, the Commission majority made only small steps in the necessary direction.

"This minority report is intended to amplify and extend these analyses from my own professional perspective as a clinical and research psychologist.

divorce and father absence

"From a scientific point of view, statistics demonstrating what now amounts to 30 years of strongly parallel increases in divorce rate, single parenting, father absence, and children's maladjustment are highly suggestive but not definitive in determining causal relations. However, it would be foolhardy and against all rules of common sense to ignore such a strong association. Moreover, a wealth of research studies have now been conducted to strengthen the conclusion that divorce, single parenting, and father absence are strongly related to adverse child and adolescent outcomes. From the perspective of child psychology, what does the accumulated research evidence conclude? First, it is abundantly clear that existing divorce procedures have not worked "in the best interests of the child." Repeatedly, in study after study since the mid- 1970's, divorced-family children have been shown to function more poorly than children from biologically intact two-parent families on a wide range of academic, social, and emotional measures. My own research studies, on the first nationwide sample of 699 children from 38 states, strongly confirm the substantial decrements in performance of divorced family children on standardized tests, self-reports, and independent ratings by parents and teachers. (e.g., Guidubaldi, 1989; Guidubaldi, 1988; Guidubaldi, Perry, & Nastasi, 1987) These results are also confirmed at two follow-up periods in subsamples from the original study — one that included 220 subjects at 2 and 3-year follow-ups and another that included 81 adolescents and young adults in a 7 and 8-year follow-up study.

This study also concluded that (a) the effects of divorce are not temporary stressors but rather long-term influences, (b) boys have more difficulties adjusting to divorce, particularly as they approach adolescence, (c) contrary to the position of some professionals (e.g., Bane, 1979) the decline in socioeconomic status after divorce is not a sufficient explanation for children's decreased performance, and (d) authoritative child-rearing style and structure in home routines such as bedtimes, mealtimes, and television viewing habits relate to better child outcomes.

One of the most striking findings was that 51 % of children from sole mother custody families see their fathers "once or twice a ear or never." In our smaller 7 and 8-year follow-up sample we found that even after an average of 11 or 12 years following the divorce event, adolescents who have good relationships with their noncustodial fathers have fewer teacher-ratings of behavior problems, fewer attention or aggression problems, higher grades in Language and Social Studies, and are less likely to abuse drugs or alcohol according to their own self-ratings.

In the only other nationwide study, Furstenberg and Nord found almost the exact percentage (50%) of father absent cases. One can speculate whether this high incidence of absence stems from fathers' selfish interests in pursuing less responsible lifestyles, or whether their parenting efforts are thwarted by restrictions imposed by custodial moms or gender biased court orders.

This interpretation is supported by Kruk (1992) who notes the most frequent reason for fathers' disengagement (90%) was obstruction of paternal access by the child's mother and her desire to break contact between father and child. Interestingly, this explanation is not even considered in the Commission's listing of possible reasons on page 14 of the majority report. Fathers also mentioned that they ceased contact because of their inability to adapt to the constraints of the visiting situation (33%). Regardless of interpretation of motives, the fact remains that sole maternal custody relates strongly to ultimate father absence. Another salient research issue is the highly replicated finding that boys fare much more poorly than girls in post-divorce households. Since more than 88 % of divorced-family children are in sole mother-custody homes, and as explained earlier, half of these have almost no contact with dads, it is clear that many boys are being reared without benefit of a same-sex parental figure.

Thus father absence may reasonably be hypothesized as an explanation for the strong gender differences in post-divorce child adjustment — a condition not easily ameliorated by the school environment which is populated by female role models for at least the first seven years of formal schooling. The relationship of father absence to child adjustment in unmarried mother households presents additional evidence for a policy of shared parenting. In our studies of urban children in special education (e.g., Guidubaldi & Duckworth, 1996), we find that 70% of children (mostly boys) with severe behavioral handicaps have no father contact at all according to the mothers' ratings. These children and adolescents are often the most disturbed or potentially dangerous students in school. One is compelled to ask how many of them would exhibit more cooperative behavior if their fathers were available and influencing their daily lives. Research summaries previously provided to Commission members document an impressive array of significant relationships between father involvement and better child adjustment for the total sample of urban children in special education, including categories such as learning disability, mental retardation, severe behavior problems, and sensory handicaps. Once again, the Commission majority failed to respond to highly pertinent data."

joint custody: a win-win proposition

"The overwhelming weight of testimony and printed material presented to the Commission supports the notion of increasing the involvement of parents in the child's, life. Our mission statement embodies this challenge to ensure that children receive not only financial support but also emotional support from both parents. We have heard consistent support for more father involvement from respected researchers and child development specialists such as Sanford Braver, Joan Kelly, Richard Warshak, Henry Biller, Nicholas Zill, and others. Why then is there still Commission opposition to a recommendation that would, by definition, increase father involvement opportunity for those seeking to maintain parenting roles after divorce?

"As Richard Warshak's testimony indicates, no study has found that joint physical custody is disadvantageous to children. Where researchers have found significant differences, they favor the joint custody arrangement. Only a few empirical studies raise any concerns at all about joint custody and these have been given an unwarranted anti joint custody "spin." These studies merit a closer look. For example, Janet Johnston's work has been cited as opposing joint custody. She notes in her article, "Court-ordered joint physical custody and frequent visitation arrangements in high-conflict divorce tend to be associated with poorer child outcomes, especially for girls" (High Conflict Divorce,1994, p. 165).

"A closer look at her definition of high conflict families reveals that she estimated the incidence from Maccoby and Mnookin's California study where 25 % of the divorcing families where judged to have high conflict, but only 10 % of these (2.5 %) show an association between joint custody/frequent visitation access and poorer child adjustment. Clearly, such an extreme population should not serve as the basis for policy that affects the welfare of the other 97.5 % of the population. Johnston, herself, acknowledges that joint physical custody and frequent visitation are not detrimental to the majority of children. She notes that, "In some cases, especially where parents are cooperative, they are more beneficial" (p. 176). Maccoby and Mnookin's work is also sometimes cited as evidence against joint custody. However, closer scrutiny of their article about joint legal custody (Albiston, Maccoby, & Mnookin, 1990) reveals no negative effects and, conversely, a positive effect between joint legal custody and decreasing discord between the parents for families in which the children visited both parents. The authors conclude that, "Thus the retention of joint legal custody as an option for its affirmation of the involvement of nonresidential parents and its potential impact on perceptions of gender roles may be warranted" (p. 177).

"In addition to Maccoby's conclusion that joint custody provides a "symbol of the expectation that both parents are to continue in their role as parents after the divorce, "we should recognize that the presumption of joint custody has another equally powerful anticipatory effect. Mindful of the fact that equality of parenting privilege will be the cornerstone of court decisions, parents are likely to be far more cooperative in pre-trial mediation, and may avoid litigation all together. If on the other hand, either of the potential litigants forecasts an advantageous position in court, their involvement in meaningful mediation may be severely compromised, and the efforts of even the most skilled mediators may be thwarted. Political extrapolations have sometimes resulted in the conclusion that where there is conflict at the time of divorce (when isn't there?) joint custody should be precluded. If this conclusion were allowed to stand, it would serve as incentive to promote conflict by those desiring sole custody. Conflict is certainly present in most divorcing situations, but it usually subsides with time. Temporary anger is common in reaction to such a powerful psychosocial stressor. It is not ordinarily indicative of pathology and should not result in an abrogation of parenting rights. Moreover, the expansion of the definition of spousal abuse has further confused the issue. Rather well defined rules of evidence pertaining to occurrences of physical abuse provide necessary safeguards against false claims, as well as protecting those who are truly victims.

"However, in recent years, more amorphous claims of "psychological abuse" have been elevated to the same level of consequence and have become widespread in divorce actions. Often rules of evidence are cast aside and the simplistic "guilty until proven innocent" orientation is exercised by confused judges who have limited ability to distinguish between truly menacing verbal behavior and harmless verbal expressions of anger (which flow both ways in marital discord). These distortions have fueled the controversy over what might otherwise appear to be an obviously fair proposition — that neither parent should lose parenting privileges or responsibilities as a result of divorce. A frequently heard rationale for sole mother custody concerns the issue of pre-divorce parenting role performance serving as a precedent for post-divorce parenting roles In response, it should be noted that during the marriage, traditional role complementary provides for efficient childrearing, wherein one of the parents usually serves as the primary bread-winner, providing for the child's food shelter, clothing, etc. while the other parent's main focus is on utilizing these resources in providing direct services for the child. Neither contribution should be denigrated in determining post-divorce childrearing privileges or responsibilities. Since both roles were essential for child welfare, since both parties may be presumed to have had at least a tacit agreement to these role divisions, and since in many families the roles are not mutually exclusive and may involve a considerable amount of overlap, the pre-divorce parenting roles should not be the basis for post-divorce parenting time and should not place either parent at a disadvantage in custody conflicts.

"Furthermore, it is blatantly clear that post-divorce lifestyles are markedly changed for all parties concerned, and a consequent redefinition of roles and privileges is essential. For example, to expect mothers to be dependent economically on their divorced spouses neglects their capabilities to become self sufficient, productive wage earners, and in fact may promote attitudes of learned helplessness. To expect fathers to continue to provide for the child's well- being through child support payments to their ex-spouses neglects the father's capacity to contribute directly to the child's well-being and may promote anger, resentment and a sense of "taxation without representation". For many fathers, the orientation is that of a second class citizen placed outside the child's mainstream, useful only as a source of continued financial support. For many mothers, this unequal post-divorce situation results in the feeling of continued economic dependency, a need to support the child on a reduced financial base since two households must now be maintained, and the inability to move forward into new employment opportunities because of the heavy childrearing burden essential in sole custody. Another argument frequently heard against joint custody is that children are unable to make transitions from one parent's home to another. No evidence is brought to bear on this assumption, and indeed ample evidence exists to support the alternative conclusion that developmental capabilities, of even young children, enable them to make healthy transitions from one environment to another (as in movement from home to daycare, baby-sitter's residence, and grandparent's homes). On what basis then, should we conclude that even young children cannot make the transition from one loving parent to another? Do the minor inconveniences outweigh the positive contributions of a highly involved caring parent?

"Considering the controversy over the issue of joint custody and the distortions of research findings in the service of preserving the sole-mother custody status quo, I asked two officials of the American Psychological Association, who gave testimony, to provide the Commission with an objective analysis of this body of research. I requested this openly in the Cleveland, Ohio Commission hearing on April 20th, and no objections were raised by other Commissioners. Following its approval by the Division 16 Operating Committee, the subsequent report was submitted on June

14, 1995 by Beth Doll, the Division Vice President for Social Council and Ethical Responsibility and Ethnic Minority Affairs. It began with the following statement:

"A search of the empirical research specific to joint custody was conducted. Major data-based studies available at the time of this review have been individually summarized and evaluated relevant to findings and adequacy of the methodology as requested. While flawless studies on such a complex subject are extremely rare as indicated by the evaluations, the goal of this report is to provide a synthesis so that the Commission's policy recommendations may be predicated on the best available empirical base. To minimize some of the confusion in such a highly charged area of study, this review focused on the weight of evidence as determined by both replication of findings and consideration of methodological rigor. This document then reviewed results from 23 studies, providing abstracts of each and summary findings according to criteria of (a) father involvement, (b) best interests of the child standard, (c) financial child support, (d) relitigation and costs to the family, and (e) parental conflict. On each of these criteria, the report supports the conclusion that joint custody is associated with favorable outcomes."

"Regrettably, this objective analysis from the world's largest organization of psychologists was ignored in our Commission meetings and in our final report. As an authoritative source of information on the social and emotional well-being of our citizenry, the APA has consistently promoted standards of gender equity. In its Council meeting in 1977, almost 20 years ago, it recognized the centrality of these issues: Be it resolved that the Council of Representatives recognizes officially and makes suitable promulgation of the fact that it is scientifically and psychologically baseless, as well as a violation of human rights, to discriminate against men because of their sex in assignment of children's custody, in adoption, in the staffing of child-care services, and personnel practices providing for parental leave in relation to childbirth and emergencies involving children and in similar laws and procedures."

references from dr. guidubaldi's report

Albistoma, C. R., Maccoby, E. E., & Mnookin, R. R. (1990). Does joint legal custody matter? Stanford Law and Policy Review, 2, 167-179

American Psychological Association. (1995). Preliminary summary: Empirical research describing outcomes of joint custody. Washington, DC.

Annie E. Casey Foundation. (1994). Kids Count Data Book.

Bane, M. J. (1976). Marital disruption and the lives of children. Journal of Social Issues, 32, 109-110.

Bennett, W. J. (1987). The role of the family in the nurture and protection of the young. American Psychologist, 42, 246-250.

Committee on the Judiciary of the United States Senate. (1975). Our Nation's schools-a report card: "A" in school violence and vandalism (Preliminary report of the Subcommittee to investigate juvenile delinquency). Washinton DC, Government Printing Office.

Furstenberg, F., Nord, C., & Zill, N. (1983). The life course of children of divorce: Marital disruption and parental contact. American Sociological Review, 48, (Oct), 656-668.

Guidubaldi, J. (1989), Differences in children's divorce adjustment across grade level and gender: A report from the NASP-Kent State nationwide project In S. Wolchik & Karoly (Eds.) Children of Divoce: Perspectives and adjustment (pp. 185-231). Lexington, MA: Lexington Books

Guidubaldi, J. (1988), The legacy of lost families: Divorce and the next generation. The World & I, Nov, 520-534.

Guidubaldi, J. (1980). The status report extended: Further elaboration's the American family. School Psychology Review, 9(4), 374-379.

Guidubaldi, J., & Duckworth J, (1996, March). Enhancing fathers' involvement in child rearing: An empirical basis for consultation and parent education, Symposium presented at the National Association of School Psychologists Annual Convention Atlanta, GA

Guidubaldi, J., Perry, J., & Nastasi, B. (1987), Growing up in a divorced family: Initial and long- term perspectives on children's adjustment In S. Oskamp (Ed.). Applied social psychological annual: Volume 7 family processes and problems: Social psychology aspects, Newbury Park, CA: Sage.

Johnston, J. R. (1994). High-Conllict Divorce. In R. E. Behrman The Future of Children 4(1) (pp.165-182), The Center for the Future of Children, The David and Lucile Packard Foundation

Kazi, N. I., & Azizun, N. I. (1994). Islam. Marriage and the Family in today's world: Interreligious colloquium, (pp. 65-74), Pontifical Council for Interreligious Dialogue,

Pontifical Council for the Family, Vatican City, Rome.

Kohlberg, L. (1976). Moral stages and moralization. In T. Lickona (Ed.), Moral development and behavior: Theory, research and social issues. New York: Holt, Rhinehart & Winston.

Kohlberg, L. (1969). Stage and sequence: The cognitive developmental approach to socialization. In D. A. Goslin (Ed.), Handbook of socialization theory and research. Chicago: Rand McNally.

Mondale, W. F. (1977). Introducing a special report: The family in trouble. Psychology Today, May, 39.

Wiley, D. (1977). Declining achievement scores: Do we need to worry? St. Louis: CEMRELL

notes & references

1. Introductory statistics
National Center for Health Statistics, Divorced Families, 1997, quoted by Dr. Rick Kuhn, Research Evaluator, Children's Rights Council

2. "A hole in the heart"
This chapter's title was inspired by the following book:
Berman, Claire. A Hole In My Heart: Adult Children of Divorce Speak Out. A Fireside book, Simon & Schuster, 1991

3. Quoted from: Dennis Guttsman, ACSW, unpublished

4. Sanford Braver, a professor of psychology at Arizona State University, completed an eight-year study on divorced fathers – the largest ever federally funded study on the subject. He found that many of the so-called facts about divorced fathers are just myths.

The book referred to is:

Braver, Sanford. Divorced Dads: Shattering the Myths. Tarcher/Putnam, 1998

5. Reference for the quote from Presiding Judge Dorothy T. Beasley, of the Georgia Court of Appeals:

"In the interest of A.R.B., a child", Georgia Court of Appeals, Case No. A93A0698, July 2, 1993. Subsequently heard by the Supreme Court of Georgia, which upheld the Court of Appeals finding that, according to public policy of Georgia, joint custody was in the best interests of children when both parents are fit.

6. Justice Ginsburg's words quoted by Jeffrey Rosen in The New York Times Magazine, October 15, 1997

7. Almost unheard of before 1970, shared parenting (joint physical custody) has grown very rapidly over the past quarter-century. Today, joint physical custody is awarded in more than one out of five divorces.

The chart on the following page is from the National Center for Health Statistics, Centers for Disease Control (14 state sample, 1989-1990; 22 state sample, 1991-1994).

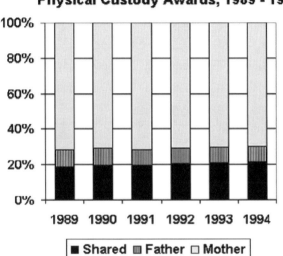

Physical Custody Awards, 1989 - 1994

■ Shared ▦ Father □ Mother

8. Statistics showing compliance child support payment based on father's custody. Source: 1988 Census "Child Support and Alimony: 1989 Series P-60, No. 173 p. 6-7. and U.S. General Accounting Office Report" GAO/HRD-92-39FS January, 1992

9. Chart of Equality vs. Power & Control based on a chart by Marg Hainer, CSW and Peggy Reubens, CSW in a workshop on domestic violence and abuse, unpublished.

10. Kubler-Ross, Elizabeth. On Death and Dying. A Touchstone book, Simon & Schuster, 1997

11. About the journey:
Campbell, Joseph. The Hero With a Thousand Faces. MJF Books, 1996.

resources

how to join with kindred spirits

Don't stay isolated simply because you don't know people who can understand what you're going through. Contact one of the associations listed below (organizations in favor of shared parenting or fathers' involvement).

Chances are, there is a groups very close to where you live: The Children's Rights Council (CRC) publishes the *International Parenting Directory of Organizations* – with a list of approximately 1,200 organizations, classified by state. This directory is about $15 and can be ordered at 800-787-KIDS.

national organizations

Children's Rights Council
"The best parent is both parents"
300 I St NE - Suite 401
Washington, DC 20002-4389
Tel. 202-547-6227
www.vix.com/crc/

American Coalition for Fathers and Children
1718 M St NW, suite 187
Washington, DC 20036
Tel. 800-978-DADS
www.acfc.org
www.erols.com/afc/

Alliance for Non-Custodial Parents' Rights (ANCPR)
P.O. Box 80438
Santa Barbara, CA 93118
www.ancpr.org

Fathers for Equal Rights, Inc
1525 Elm St, Suite 3100
Dallas TX 75201
Tel. 214-953-2233
www.fathers4kids.org

Fathers' Resource Center
c/o Prevention Alliance
430 Oak Grove St, #B3

Minneapolis, MN 55403
Tel. 612-874-1509
www.parentsplace.com/readroom/frc/index.html

Fathers Rights and Equality Exchange
3140 de la Cruz Blvd, Suite 200
Santa Clara, CA 95054
1-500-FOR DADS
www.vix.com/free/

Joint Custody Association (JCA)
10606 Wilkins Ave.
Los Angeles, CA 90024
Tel. 310-474-4859
Information and advocacy for joint custody.
This association has been instrumental in putting shared
parenting into law in many states.

Men's Defense Association
17854 Lyons St NE
Forest Lake MN 55025-8854
Tel. 612-464-7887
www.mensdefense.org

Men's Health Network
P.O. Box 770
Washington, DC 20044
Tel. 202-543-6461
www.menshealthnetwork.org

National Congress for Fathers and Children (NCFC)
Communication and Data Center
PO Box 6053
Kansas City, KS 66106-0053
1-800-733-DADS
www.sound.net/~ncfcdad

Non-Custodial Parents' Resource Center
PO BOX 742
Farmerville, LA 71241
Tel. 318-368-6232
www.bayou.com/~ncprc/

for grandparents and stepparents

Grandparents Rights in New Strength (GRINS)
689 Country Road 5
Corunna, IN 46730-9760
Tel. 219-281-2384

Stepfamily Association of America
650 J St, Suite 205
Lincoln, NE 68508
Tel. 402-477-7837
www.stepfam.org

to find a mediator

Academy of Family Mediators (AFM)
4 Militia Dr

Lexington, MA 02173-4705
Tel. 781-674-2663
www.mediators.org
The leading organization in the U.S. that trains
family/divorce mediators. Provides referrals to mediators
nationwide.

American Arbitration Association
140 W 51st Street. New York, NY 10020
Tel: 212-484-4000
www.adr.org
The American Arbitration Association provides a free, confi-
dential referral service of arbitrators and mediators.

for legal help:

Several of the national organizations listed at the beginning
of this section offer some form of assistance – bookstore, listing of the applicable laws and statutes, forms, discussion
groups that allow members to learn from each other's experience…
In addition, the following may be helpful for people who are
representing themselves ("pro se") or who wish to get more
familiar with the legal issues to better understand what their
lawyers are doing.

American Pro Se Association
1441 Prospect Avenue, Plainfield, NJ 07060
Tel. 908-753-4516. Fax: 908-753-2599
www.legalhelp.org

www.divorcenet.com
provides summaries of divorce laws in all 50 states.
Also full of information and useful links:
- www.findlaw.com
- www.internetlawyer.com

Virginia's Regent University has a page about legal listservs
(discussion groups you can be part of as an active or passive
member):
www.regent.edu/lawlib/list-law.html

for couple therapy

American Association for Marriage and Family Therapy
(AAMFT)
1133 15th St. NW Suite 300
Washington, DC 20005-2170
Tel. 202-452-0109
www.amft.org
Professional organization of marriage and family therapists
with 23,000 members in the U. S. and Canada. Operates a
referral service (1-800-374-2638; soon also on the internet).

for more resources

Men's Issues page
http://www.vix.com/pub/men

Men's Health Network Reference Library
http://www.menshealthnetwork.org/library/libraryTOC.html

acknowledgments

Writing a book means, among other things, dealing with a paradox. One starts such an endeavor out of a passionate desire to communicate with others. Yet, the process of writing is essentially a solitary endeavor.

I have been very fortunate to find a lot of support. Throughout the long process of writing, and re-writing, and re-writing yet again… many people read the various drafts, commented on them, gave me encouragement as well constructive criticism and nudged me to keep going deeper.

Having finally completed the book, I am very happy about the finished product. I am proud of what I've done. But I'm very aware that the result is not the fruit of a solitary effort. In fact, I am in awe of how much help I have received. I am very touched by how much support there has been out there. There's no way that a few words at the back of this book can do justice to all those who have contributed so much in so many ways.

I am deeply indebted to Leighton Chong, Roddy Duchesne, John Guarnaschelli, Dennis Guttsman, Ken Neumann, Peggy Reubens (my wife) and Diane Yale for all the work they did in analyzing the manuscripts in terms of structure and contents, and coming up with suggestions.

I am especially grateful to Leighton Chong, John Guarnaschelli and Diane Yale – who essentially each performed the function of a talented editor, keeping track of the big picture while paying attention to the actual contents.

It was wonderful to receive feedback on the manuscripts from such readers as Travis Ballard, Barry Berkman, Kim Boedecker-Frey, Neal Brodsky, Adrian Buckmaster, Jan Cohen, Jim Cook, Marcel Duclos, Paul Finger, Mary Giuffra, Rick Kuhn, David Levy, Milton Louvaris, Jayne Major, Jeffrey Nichols, Judi Price, Bea and Ned Reubens, Joe Sahid, Gary Seiden, Ed Stephens, Bob Stien, Thomas Thornton, John Vitullo, Doug Waldmann, Monty Weinstein, Howard Yagerman.

For the sections on parenting, I am indebted to the ideas of Dr. Ron Taffel – a leading family therapist and author. Thank you, Dr. Taffel, for sharing your ideas so generously.

I also want to acknowledge at least some of the people to whom I owe my training in psychotherapy – people whose help was not directly related to this book, but without whom the book would not be what it is: Stuart Black, Michael

THE DIVORCED FATHER'S JOURNEY

Hungerman, Joyce Livingston, John Pierrakos, Gobi Stromberg of the Institute of Core Energetics; and Yvonne Agazarian, Fran Carter, Jon McCormick of the Systems Centered Training Institute.

Thanks to Aldo Coppelli, Mark Greenberg, Claudie Poulain, Jean-Louis Prengel, Joan and Mike Sloser for their helpful comments on the cover design.

dear reader of this book

You can get in touch with other divorced fathers at www.divorcedfather.com or www.stilladad.com

I would like to hear from you – what this book has meant to you, and how it relates to your experience.

You can reach me by e-mail:
serge-prengel@stilladad.com
or by regular mail:
Serge Prengel,
c/o Mission Creative Energy
27 W 24th St (# 603)
New York, NY 10010

You can also write to the author of the foreword:
Diane Yale
4465 Douglas Avenue
Bronx, New York 10471-3523